Understanding the Asian Indian Diaspora and Mental Health

Cognella Series on Advances in Culture, Race, and Ethnicity

Understanding the Asian Indian Diaspora and Mental Health

Liberation from Western Frameworks

SONIA AMIN AND PRIYA BANSAL

Series edited by Miguel Gallardo, Psy.D.; Allen Ivey, Ed.D., ABPP; Joseph E. Trimble, Ph.D.; Norweeta G. Milburn, Ph.D.; and Sumie Okazaki, Ph.D.

cognella

SAN DIEGO

Bassim Hamadeh, CEO and Publisher
Amy Smith, Senior Project Editor
Rachel Kahn, Production Editor
Jess Estrella, Senior Graphic Designer
Kylie Bartolome, Licensing Associate
Natalie Piccotti, Director of Marketing
Kassie Graves, Senior Vice President, Editorial
Jamie Giganti, Director of Academic Publishing

3970 Sorrento Valley Blvd., Ste. 500, San Diego, CA 92121

Brief Contents

Detailed Contents

Preface

The past few decades have witnessed a rapid increase in the immigration of Asians of Indian descent to the United States. This has predicated a need to understand the various sociocultural and political experiences that shape the identity development and mental health experiences of this population, particularly given their rising risk of mental health concerns. This book was born out of an attempt to give voice to our personal and collective experiences, which we did not read about or have access to growing up. American society dictates what an American looks like by stipulating what is "acceptable" behavior, who is allowed to claim space or have their voice heard, and which indigenous or heritage cultural practices are embraced (i.e., appropriated) versus not. Adjustments that people make in order to mold to American society often translate into shedding old world traditions, hiding aspects of one's identity or experiences, and/or negotiating their identity to fit into American spaces. These painful experiences are often cloaked: an invisible curtain that hides the many battles that Asian Indian people and many other racial and ethnic minority communities experience as they attempt to survive and thrive in American society. In writing this book, we are pulling aside the curtain—directly naming and examining systems of oppression that color the experiences of Asian Indians in this country.

Current literature tends to homogenize Asian Indians with other groups (e.g., Asian Americans) and emphasizes the association between mental health experiences and culture in a general sense. Missing from the literature is a critical assessment of how various interlocking systems of oppression—both within the United States and in India—collectively influence Asian Indian people's experiences in the United States. Although we recognize that there has been a substantial shift across mental health fields toward social justice, liberation, and decolonization, we have noticed that the literature is lacking instruction on how to apply these philosophies in practice. Thus, the central objectives of this book are (a) to provide an overview of three systems of inequality that largely shape the mental health experiences of Asian Indians in the United States, (b) to critically analyze shortcomings of Western models of psychological healing, and (c) to help bridge the gap between theory and practice with regard to liberation and decolonization in psychotherapeutic clinical work.

We believe three particular systems of inequality—racism, the Indian caste system, and patriarchy—have been the most influential in determining how the Asian Indian community negotiates, interacts with, and adapts to experiences of marginalization and privilege. In order to help illustrate the intersectional experiences of Asian Indian people as they collide with these systems, didactic discussions about these systems of inequality are interwoven with in-depth vignettes of two hypothetical clients receiving mental health services, whose stories were informed by our own personal and professional experiences as well as conversations with various members of the Asian Indian diasporic community.

In Chapter 1, we help you settle into the book through an introduction to identity and guided reflections. We then contextualize racism, the caste system, and patriarchy in their transnational histories and provide information you can continue to refer back to as you journey through the rest of the chapters. Chapters 2–4 present a deeper dive into each system of oppression respectively, and we demonstrate how two hypothetical clients—Anaisha and Samar—are impacted by each. Discussing the same two cases throughout the book allows for a rich and multidimensional perspective on the relationship between systems of oppression and mental health. In these chapters, we provide recommendations for topics that clinicians should be mindful to explore, as well as examples of language that clinicians might use to do so. In the final chapter, we invite you to engage in a critical reflection of the limitations and failures of traditional Western therapeutic approaches and training programs. After a didactic discussion on non-Western, ancient indigenous healing practices, we provide guidelines for clinicians to develop their own therapeutic philosophies grounded in the principle that psychological healing necessitates liberation from systems of oppression.

Acknowledgments

Two years ago, neither of us would have imagined that we would be writing this book together, and yet here we are. A true labor of love, this text is reflective of all that we have gained from those who came before us—our families, mentors, guides, friends, peers, clients, and community members. Writing this book has allowed us to give voice to our ancestral histories and community's experiences and helped deepen our understanding of our own cultural practices. There are many people who have helped shape both the content and structure of the book and to whom we would like to extend our deepest gratitude. First, we would like to thank Dr. Sumie Okazaki for seeing us and our community's experiences as important enough to be written about and for allowing us the space to write what came from our hearts. We would also like to thank Kassie Graves and Amy Smith, our wonderful editors, for your unwavering faith and continuous encouragement throughout the writing of this book.

We would like to extend special gratitude to Pooja Mamidanna for your contributions in the development of the book proposal; much of our early excitement about this project was colored by dialogues we were able to have with you, and we are deeply appreciative. In particular, we thank you for your engagement with us around topics of diversity in the Asian Indian diaspora, differences across migration stories, and navigating imposter syndrome.

To the various anonymous members of our Asian Indian diasporic community who shared with us your histories, stories, and experiences: your words have significantly shaped the content of this book and the cases described here. We sincerely thank you for your trust, vulnerability, and willingness to share so much of yourselves with us.

We would like to give special thanks to Shanta Jambotkar, LCSW, and Dr. Sayali Amarapurkar, executive director of AshaUSA, for your valuable reflections and thoughts on our book. We also thank Kusha Murarka, PsyD, for your provocative discussions and reflections around social justice in South Asian communities that have significantly influenced the tenderness and care given to specific areas of the book.

We are extremely grateful to the other individuals who took the time and energy to offer thoughts and feedback on our manuscript. You are professors, mental health professionals, innovators, critical thinkers, and people within and outside of the Asian Indian diaspora. You engaged with the material from your diverse perspectives, asked questions, and raised thoughtful discussions; ultimately, your feedback was essential in shaping the final version of this book.

Finally, we are deeply thankful to our families and friends, who believed in us and supported us in this project from the very beginning when we didn't even know we would be writing a book.

1

Navigating Storms: Systems of Inequality

Introduction

The Asian Indian diaspora refers to people whose ancestry can be traced back to the Indian subcontinent of Asia. Historically, the Indian subcontinent has included both present-day India and its surrounding countries; therefore, people's degrees of identification with the diaspora may vary based on their ancestral histories and complex historical and political dynamics. Diasporas have existed around the world for a very long time, and Asian Indians who reside in the United States are incredibly diverse in the experiences and paths that have led them here. Some families immigrated here directly from India, while others have lived in other countries along the way, sometimes for generations. Some members of the diaspora are just beginning to establish their lives here and may not yet be accompanied by much of their family. The diaspora in the United States also includes people who were born here. Across these diverse experiences, there is a sense of cohesion both in the diaspora's cultural origins and in what it is like for them to navigate life in the United States. Understanding mental health within the Asian Indian diaspora in this country involves being mindful of both the heterogeneity and the unity among its people.

What is it like to be an Asian Indian person in the United States? It is like standing in a storm.

We stand with our feet in the earth, soil unfamiliar but soil just the same, trying to be trees. Why? We use these words to describe belonging: connected, secure. We use these words to describe security: grounded, rooted. It is human to crave belonging and security; humans are social beings, and building (and maintaining) connections is how we thrive. We seek to deepen our roots, expand our networks, and establish our communities. In these ways, trees are a literal, visual representation of our human desires.

There are several barriers we can face to building sustainable communities. Sometimes, we are transplanted and it takes time, or the soil is dry and it takes energy. For some, there are environmental factors: persistent clouds that block nutrients from the sun, overbearing rain that threatens to wash us out, or forceful winds that knock us down. And sometimes, there is a storm, which is multifaceted: more than just clouds, rain, and wind, but rather the culmination of all of these elements—when rain turns to downpour, or wind clashes clouds.

What is it like to be an Asian Indian person in the United States? It is like being a tree in a persistent storm. There are multiple systems of inequality that underlie U.S. society, each of them more or less salient in the lives of individuals based on the identities with which they navigate the world. Many people think of **racism** first, as race is often highlighted in this country as a divider of groups and an undercurrent of conflict. Asian Indians struggle against nuanced oppression under White supremacy. There is also the Indian **caste system**, prevalent in the United States as well as in India, which can tear Asian Indian communities apart and intertwine with racism in unique and damaging ways. Finally, there is **patriarchy**, under which there are multiple subsystems that target noncisgender people, nonheterosexual people, and women. Asian Indians in the United States navigate the oppression of patriarchy from both a Western lens and an Indian one, balancing both where they overlap and conflict. In this book, we focus specifically on these three systems of oppression because we feel they significantly shape the mental health experiences of the Asian Indian diaspora in the United States.

A Personal Note

By now, you have gathered that asking what it is like to be an Asian Indian person in the United States is a deceptively simple question. In reflecting upon having been asked this question throughout our respective lives, we—Sonia and Priya—uncover nuances and layers that make it difficult to address. For instance, it sometimes feels as if we carry the weight of describing our experiences as universal to the Asian Indian diaspora in the United States—an impossible task. In reflecting about just our own identities, we notice there are just as many differences as there are similarities; while we are both educated, Asian Indian, cisgender women, we also have different immigration experiences, sexualities, castes, and family systems. All of these variables influence what it is like to be us, and we feel there is no single answer to the question.

On the other hand, we live in a society that necessitates acknowledging that Asian Indian individuals have some experiences that are, at the very least, universally different from that of the majority, which is commonly considered to be the Western, White population. The need to acknowledge that the cultural complexity within identities leads to different experiences, and subsequently to give voice to the experiences of those who differ from the majority, is what birthed multicultural fields of study. We feel a responsibility to give voice to the Asian Indian diaspora in the United States.

It is important for us to be intentional about the questions we are asking, and also what we are *not* asking or answering. We are cognizant that in many social sciences and subfields, the move toward **multicultural competence** is coupled with a push to familiarize ourselves with facets of different cultures so as to be more aware and therefore functional with the people with whom we work. This book is not about Asian Indian culture. As much as you may learn about the culture through the narrative of this book, we also implore you to remain cognizant about the lens through which this book is written: the focus is the storm. What an Asian Indian person is like is different from what it is like for an Asian Indian person to exist in the United States, and here we focus on the latter. We focus on the experiences and the factors that inform them. As psychotherapists, we also return frequently to mental health correlates and psychological impacts of living within systems of oppression. Standing in a storm is difficult, and it is harmful. Thus, we have crafted this book from the perspective of both subject and audience: as Asian Indians and as people in helping professions seeking to foster hope, healing, and empowerment for Asian Indians in the United States.

Our endeavor to give voice to the Asian Indian diaspora is limited here by the perspectives of our identities, experiences, and research. There are inevitably biases and gaps in the way this book is written because the two of us alone are not representative of the vast diversity of identities held by the Asian Indian diaspora. Throughout our writing process, we consulted with other members of the Asian Indian diasporic community, engaged in dialogues, and heard and incorporated their stories. However, we are still mindful that the guidance we provide for you to reflect on the intersectionality of multiple identities—privileged and marginalized—comes from a relatively privileged perspective.

On Identity

We would be remiss to overlook that Asian Indians are heterogeneous; there are a myriad of identities that inform their life experiences. Thus, it follows that systems of inequality affect and manifest for them in different ways. For example, an individual's experience with race, caste, and patriarchy as an Asian Indian may be unique in some ways if they also identify as a woman. How might their experience be if they are Muslim, or queer, or **Dalit**,[1] or if they hold all of these identities at once? Rather than dissecting each identity, it is important to think about what each means in context. We encourage you to take an environmental approach to context; search also outside of the gender, religion, caste, sexual orientation, and other identities that a person holds. Which spaces do they occupy? Who is in their environment? What is the big picture of their life?

It is much easier said than done to maintain a focus broader than identity-level when the process for beginning to understand an experience has for so long been somewhat of a "divide and conquer" method based on identities. When we begin to explore what it is like to hold a particular identity or set of identities, we arrive at an inevitable paradox. There are very real human experiences that are explicitly tied to certain identities, such as **privilege**, **marginalization**, and societal expectations; at the same time, generalization easily falls into the realm of unfairness, where it becomes unwarranted to assume that everyone who holds a particular identity is the same. So, how do we find the balance between asking important questions and refraining from making incorrect and potentially harmful generalizations?

Unfortunately, we do not have a clear answer to this question, so we invite you to do some critical thinking with us. "Divide and conquer" is a colonialist ideology and has for centuries guided psychological fields of study. As the fields centered and normalized European experiences, they marginalized and pathologized others. That we are now shining a light on Asian Indian lives in the United States is a response to this colonial harm that has created systems in which people are categorized and ranked. In many ways, though, we are forced to challenge the systems from the inside out. In order to properly give voice to Asian Indians, to reclaim experiences outside of what has been dictated by the creators of our fields, we must call attention to how Asian Indians differ from what has for so long been considered the "norm"; however, doing so in some ways reinforces the use of identities, labels, and categories.

Rather than assessing disembodied identity labels throughout this book, we have endeavored instead to share with you realistic—albeit fictional—people. Instead of comprehensively exploring different identities and how they may change individuals' experiences within systems of oppression, we instead focus on illustrating the lives of two unique people in order to show what can be involved with understanding the Asian Indian diaspora and their mental health. In the rest of this chapter, we provide histories and overviews of three systems of inequality—racism, casteism, and patriarchy—pertaining to the Asian Indian diaspora in the United States. We then introduce two case studies of fictional Asian Indian mental health counseling clients. In subsequent chapters, we engage in deep exploration of cultural socialization and mental health considerations related to each system of inequality.

A Reflection Exercise

We invite you to consider your own positionality as you navigate this book. Take a moment to situate yourself and your identities: Who are you? Which of your cultural identities (gender, race, immigration status, sexual orientation, and a myriad of others) are most salient for you? In which areas of your life do you hold privilege or carry the weight of marginalization? Consider how these experiences have shaped who you are today.

There may be certain expectations you have of this text. If you are knowledgeable of Asian Indian history or are part of the diaspora, the factual information in this book may read as familiar, old news. We urge you, though, not to limit your open mind or capacity to be surprised. Instead, see how you can weave your own narrative into the chapters of this book: How does your positionality inform what you gain from the text?

Or, perhaps this is the first time you have given much thought to the Asian Indian diaspora, or the first time you are learning of these words, these people. Being positioned outside of the diaspora, it may feel overwhelming to dive so deeply into the rich and diverse history and experiences of this group—there is a lot to learn. But while Asian Indians are a unique group with a colorful cultural history, the systems of oppression they navigate in the United States are not exclusive to them. Regardless of your positionality, you may experience a range of emotional reactions to this text because it may conflict with your own worldviews and things you have been taught within Western frameworks. Part of liberation involves noticing your emotions and considering the barriers that are coming up for you as you progress through this book. We hope that through continued introspection in your journey through this book, you will gain insights into the complexities of systems of oppression, the heterogeneity of mental health experiences, and the importance of liberation from Western frameworks of psychology.

Racism: The Clouds

Arguably, immigration has both directly and indirectly shaped the identity development of people who reside in the United States. Most individuals in the United States have ancestors who participated in immigration, either by choice, force, or enslavement; thus, their history includes establishing identities in the Americas by finding a balance between maintaining elements of their previous lives abroad and creating new lives here. This negotiation between old and new life, **acculturation**, and **assimilation** has historically been the way immigration and community establishment have been taught in U.S. history courses. Often overlooked in these courses are the underlying and intersecting factors such as race, ethnicity, culture, religion, and many more identity variables that determine the true and greatly complex experience of immigration and its connection with mental health. For People of Color, including Asian Indians, the connection between immigration and mental health cannot be adequately understood without acknowledging the influence of White supremacy and the racism it breeds.

White Supremacy in U.S. History

Although they have always lived in the Americas, Native American and Indigenous families were affected by the first wave of European immigration, colonialism, and genocide. Their forced negotiation with Whiteness across time, including defining their group identity based in part on their fight for survival, has been a significant factor in ethnic and cultural identity development for Indigenous communities (Horse (Kiowa), 2005). Latinx immigrants and African Americans who identify as slave descendants have their own volatile histories, and their ethnic and cultural identity development has been similarly influenced by negotiation with Whiteness and their fight for racial justice in a system of White supremacy (Chavez-Dueñas et al., 2019; Du Bois, 1903). It is important to note that while communities of color share the burden of having their development stunted or negotiated by White supremacy, the manifestation of this struggle is highly varied across ethnic groups. In order to truly understand how and why immigration is important to identity development for Asian Indians, a deeper dive into their history is warranted.

White Supremacy in U.S. Asian Indian History

The racial categorization of Asian Indians during the first half of the 20th century was inconsistent. While East Asian (e.g., Chinese American, Japanese American) subgroups were losing their fight for citizenship and the rights to be in the United States, immigrants from India were obtaining legal naturalization. At the time,

U.S. law stated that naturalization could only be granted to "free white persons," a requirement they deemed East Asians did not meet; however, Asian Indians were at the time considered anthropologically Caucasian, thus "different" from other Asian subgroups and theoretically eligible for naturalization (Hess, 1969; Shah, 1999). Concurrently, due to this racially charged distinction between Asian Indians and East Asians, Asian Indians were somewhat protected from severe maltreatment and discrimination inflicted by explicitly anti-Asian laws such as the Chinese Exclusion Act (1882). These differences in experiences between Asian Indians and East Asians in the United States illustrates how early tensions between racial minority groups were created by and because of White supremacy. For example, in 1923, a Sikh man named Bhagat Singh Thind fought the United States Supreme Court for naturalization rights on a platform that dehumanized East Asians by claiming that Asian Indians were superior based on their Caucasian status, which placed them closer to Whiteness in the racial hierarchy.

United States v. Bhagat Singh Thind (1923) ultimately classified Asian Indians as "Asian," thus subjecting them to other existing anti-Asian laws. Further, as a result of this decision, citizenship was revoked for many Asian Indians who had previously been granted naturalization. Thus, there is a history of cognitive dissonance for Asian Indians regarding how they are perceived and treated in the United States; at times, they have been acknowledged as a unique group, and other times, as part of a pan-ethnic Asian group.

Even today, this cognitive dissonance and the impact of White supremacy is reflected in the "both-and" identity held by Asian Indians in the United States; Asian Indians tend to be caught in the middle of the racial hierarchy, thus balancing experiences of both privilege and marginalization at the same time (Daga & Raval, 2018). Take, for example, the creation of the **model minority myth**, to which Asian Indians are subjected in the same ways as other Asian subgroups. The term and concept of the model minority was originally invented to describe Japanese people who managed to succeed in the economy after surviving American internment camps during World War II (Petersen, 1966), and has since expanded to encompass multiple Asian subgroups. Today, the model minority myth perpetuates stereotypes that Asian individuals are more successful, educated, or assimilated into American society than other racial minorities. Sometimes, the model minority myth refers to Asian individuals' perceived success compared to American society at large. While the idea that Asians are more successful than others has been shown statistically to be untrue, the model minority myth also perpetuates the idea that Asian individuals are successful because they're Asian or because Asian cultures place high value on achieving success, education, and money. This is also a broad and unfair generalization that has many consequences, including placing an expectation of success on Asian individuals and dismissing any success they do achieve as being due to their race. For Asian Indians, the saliency of the model minority concept in their identity development emerges as an effect of immigration patterns controlled by U.S. immigration policy. Historically, legal immigration to the United States was limited based on education and professional qualifications, skewing characteristics of the population of Asian Indians in the United States and contributing to stereotypes that this group is highly educated and successful. Subsequent generations of Asian Indians are then held to the same societal expectations of success despite marginalization—an unfounded and unfair stereotype that clarifies the model minority concept as a myth and has several implications for the mental health of those impacted by the label (Tummala-Narra et al., 2016). Research today shows that the pressures Asian Indians experience are grounded in both societal and intracommunity expectations (Bansal, 2020).

Although Asian Indians are subjected to this perception in the United States that they are high-achieving minorities that should serve as a model for other racial groups, they also experience explicit discrimination and racism. Some experienced racism is White supremacist xenophobia grounded in the belief that anyone who is not White is inferior. Other experiences of racism increased after the September 11, 2001, terrorist attacks. Asian Indians' intersecting identity variables such as religion and physical presentation place them at risk of targeted racism specifically related to terrorism (Iyer, 2015). This type of fear and anger-based discrimination against Asian Indians has risen further since the 2016 presidential election, with the implementation of various governmental policies negatively targeting Asian Indian students, immigrants, and their families.

Being Careful When We Talk About Asian Indian Immigration

Oftentimes when we consider what Asian Indian immigration to the United States has historically looked like, we think about the Immigration and Naturalization Act of 1965, which led to the largest wave of immigration from India; this immigration wave consisted primarily of highly skilled and educated individuals who met the quota that the United States was looking for at the time. However, individuals from India and broader South Asia have been immigrating to the United States since the late 1800s. The regions of South Asia that today are divided into India, West Bengal, Pakistan, and Bangladesh were once one region. When we talk about immigration history and its impact on Asian Indian mental health and identity development, it is important to also consider the heterogeneity of experiences of individuals from the South Asian region generally, as this heterogeneity and related impacts are reflected in the immigrant population in the United States.

The United States began controlling and barring immigration from Asian countries in the late 1800s. The Page Act of 1875 and the Chinese Exclusion Act of 1882 were established to prohibit primarily Chinese and Japanese immigration. This was followed by the Immigration Act of 1917—also known as the Asiatic Barred Zone Act—which imposed literacy evaluations on immigrants and barred immigration of individuals from East Asia, Central Asia, Southeast Asia, the Middle East, and the Indian Subcontinent. This was replaced by the Immigration Act of 1924, which, while lifting bars, imposed quotas for immigration from Asian countries. Meanwhile, between the 1880s and 1950s, working-class Muslim men from West Bengal and Bangladesh were immigrating to the United States in defiance of the exclusion laws; they found homes within Black and Puerto Rican communities, intermarried, and established new lives. It is their stories that some have named as "lost" among the stereotypes and typical image of South Asian or Asian Indian immigration. Stories of these communities can be found in *Bengali Harlem and the Lost Histories of South Asian America* by Vivek Bald (2013) and a related documentary.

Acknowledging this heterogeneity of immigration among Asian Indians and people from neighboring regions is important not only to capture the nuance of experiences within this otherwise homogenized group, but also to note a departure from the common notion that Asian Indians are a group somehow separate from other racial minorities in the United States. As illustrated in the previous section, Asian Indians are often **triangulated** in the United States framework of racial hierarchy (Kim, 1999), seen as inferior to White people but superior to (or different from) other racial minorities. If we exclusively conceptualize Asian Indians in this way, we erase the ways in which Asian communities and other racial minority communities have blended, such as with Bengali Harlem.

Generational Differences: Indirect Impact of Immigration

Some Asian Indians who immigrate to the United States retain their identities as Asian Indians despite their change of physical location, while others may adopt the label "Indian," "Asian Indian American," "Indian American," or "American." How a person chooses to identify or label themselves—their personal sense of identity—is generally related to a group identity, something that has emerged from collective or shared experiences with other people. For individuals who were born outside of the United States, the process of finding new groups of people in the United States with whom they find commonality, and adjusting their personal identities to reflect these new experiences, is called *acculturation* (Berry, 2006; Chun et al., 2003). In this process, individuals begin with an ethnic identity grounded in shared experiences with others from their home countries and slowly adjust how they identify in accordance with accumulating new shared experiences after immigration with people in the United States. In this way, someone who immigrated from India may initially identify as "Asian Indian" but may eventually begin to identify as "Indian American" if they interact with a lot of people in the United States who identify as Indian American and find commonalities with them. On the other hand, they may retain their identity as "Asian Indian" if the people they interact with and find commonalities with also identify as Asian Indian.

However, racial identity development may be less linear and a little more muddled for individuals who are born in the United States and who are not White. Second-generation immigrants—people born in the United States who are children of immigrants—often grow up caught between two different communities: at home, they interact with immigrants (i.e., their parents or family), while in other aspects of life, such as work and school, they interact with non-Asian Indians. Given the importance of community in identity development, balancing such different environments can be extremely challenging. Some researchers have noted that this challenge paints a unique opportunity for second-generation immigrants to "make the best of both worlds"; however, for many, it's not that simple (Bacon, 1999; Rajiva, 2006). Second-generation immigrants may find value in the shared experience of the struggle of being caught between two worlds. In this way, generational status could be especially salient or important for some people when they think about their identities.

Oftentimes, being a non-Black Person of Color is perceived in the United States as an external, physically clear connection to immigration. If a person is not White and not Black, it is often assumed that they were not born in the United States or that their family is not American. Furthermore, race categorization in the United States is linked to country of origin only for non-Black People of Color; this means that (e.g., on census surveys) children of immigrants from India would likely identify their race as "Asian," while White children of immigrants would identify their race as "White." In this way, children of Asian Indian immigrants and subsequent generations of individuals in the United States always carry immigration as part of their identities. It is difficult for them to simply identify as "American" because they are often not perceived that way by society; at the same time, they may not identify simply as "Asian Indian" either, because the label may not feel accurate for someone born in the United States. For first-generation immigrants—people who were not born in the United States—these assumptions based on race are a constant reminder that they are not "from" this country and ultimately serve as racist implications that they do not "belong" here. As non-Black People of Color, Asian Indians are constantly identified as outsiders in a country in which they are trying to establish their lives.

Othering as a Reaction to Discrimination

Plenty of research has been published illustrating the negative psychological consequences of discrimination such as racism (Garcia et al., 2019; Miller et al., 2011; Museus & Park, 2015), the structure of how systems of oppression are continually perpetuated; that is, history repeats itself. What is important to think about here, when attempting to understand what it is like to be an Asian Indian person in the United States, is how the impacts of discrimination fit into the larger picture of the both-and experience detailed above. How might a person react to perpetual experiences of discrimination within a system where they are both good and bad, both homogenous and unique?

A natural reaction might be to try to distance oneself from identity variables (and associated groups of people) that are linked with discrimination—a phenomenon that has been described in social sciences research as *othering* (Schwalbe et al., 2000). There are many ways and reasons to do this. For example, a person can distance themselves from negatively perceived identities by perpetuating discrimination against others who hold those identities; taking race as an example, reflect on the *United States v. Bhagat Singh Thind* case. The foundation of Thind's case was that East Asians are inferior to Whites and that Asian Indians are equivalent to Whites—superior to East Asians—and therefore deserving of naturalization rights. In addition to viewing this case as clearly problematic in its implications and treatment of East Asians, we must also consider the reasons behind Thind's position: self-preservation within a system of racial hierarchy in which he was subjected to injustice.

Another form of othering is more implicit—an internal process rather than an explicit, external one, and what Schwalbe et al. (2000) describe as the "creation of a powerful virtual self." In this type of othering, people move away from the reality of marginalization by imagining and endorsing a hypothetical, idealized image of themselves. In simpler terms, it is like putting on a front. It is a type of façade to create the impression that a person is more well-respected in society than they really are—or that they are less marginalized than they really are—as a way to protect against the pain that comes with experiencing discrimination. A poignant example of this for Asian Indians involves the model minority myth, which is perceived by many as a positive stereotype, an image for which people should strive. Many people who are affected by the myth internalize its messages and stereotypes, and, in turn, endorse the stereotypes as reflective of a general truth (Wong et al., 1998). Because the model minority myth paints certain minorities (usually people of Asian descent, like Asian Indians) in an extremely positive light in comparison to other racial minorities, Asian Indians can accept and endorse the myth to achieve a moral high ground without actively oppressing other groups of people. Further, while the model minority myth has been shown in research to be associated with increases in psychological distress (Chan & Mendoza-Denton, 2008; Gupta et al., 2011), there is also research that indicates its correlation with less psychological distress, meaning that some people who internalize model minority stereotypes associate them with better mental health (Chang, 2017; Gupta et al., 2011). We can conceptualize these examples as reflections of how positive impressions associated with the model minority myth may be a protective factor for Asian Indians against negative or painful experiences such as psychological distress and racist discrimination.

A third type of othering as a reaction to racism employs the offensive nature of perpetuating discrimination against members within one's own marginalized group. In the context of race, this is what some researchers have referred to as *internalized racism* (Osajima, 1993; Pyke, 2010; Schwalbe et al., 2000). In this type of othering, people protect themselves by exhibiting defenses against their own marginalized identities, thus creating distance between themselves and discrimination. For example, a woman might state that she is "not like other girls" because of negative stereotypes associated with being female; or an Asian Indian individual might exhibit racism against other Asian Indians or state that they do not identify with Asian Indians because of negative perceptions of that group, in order to increase their own chances of being accepted by the White majority. While people experiencing this type of reaction to discrimination can resist the "negative" perceptions of their identity, they also inadvertently perpetuate inequality and hierarchy by considering some identities to be more superior than others, and in particular, by considering aspects of their own identity to be inferior.

Racism and Mental Health

Asian Indians who immigrated to the United States were forced to conform to and survive within a Western framework grounded in White supremacy, a system of oppression. Even today, individuals of Asian Indian heritage who are born in the United States are exposed to this system of hierarchy in which they are marginalized. These experiences—of being discriminated against, being forced into a racially triangulated role in American society, and being perpetually associated with immigration even if they were born in the United States—significantly shape the ways in which Asian Indians learn to conceptualize themselves and their relationships with others. This, in turn, has a number of implications for mental health. For example, Asian Indians might develop an inferiority complex, in which perpetual marginalization reinforces that they are not "good enough" to be accepted, no matter how much they other or separate themselves from the negative perceptions of their marginalized identities (Nikalje & Çiftçi, 2021). Asian Indians may also feel a lack of belonging in their communities: because of racial triangulation and differences in immigration history, they may not feel entirely accepted by White people, by other racial minorities, or in American society in general; because of the ways in which othering as a reaction to discrimination leads to intra-ethnic division, they also may not feel entirely accepted among other Asian Indians. Research has shown that developing a personal and group identity, and feeling accepted by other people, is important for well-being (Ibrahim et al., 1997; Iwamoto & Liu, 2010; Tajfel & Turner, 1979); thus, barriers against doing so have negative implications for mental health. The threat of a lack of group acceptance and its impact on mental health is, of course, not a new concept—nor is it exclusive to Asian Indians. Even in Western culture, being ostracized, left out, bullied, and going through the process of finding community are common and normal aspects of growing up. However, for Asian Indians in the United States, these experiences occur in some form in nearly all of their environments, both within and outside of their homes, within their families and in society in general. Thus, where identity development can be an affirming and freeing process for many people as they figure out who they are, it can be an incredibly isolating process for Asian Indians in the United States.

Heterogeneity of Discrimination Experiences

Asian Indians may have different experiences of racism based on their physical appearance. Recall our brief mention of how racism against Asian Indians has changed over the years, particularly after the September 11, 2001, terrorist attacks. Since then, people who identify as Muslim have been the targets of serious and dangerous racist attacks; further, people who do not identify as Muslim but who are perceived in Western society to be different or less culturally assimilated than others, such as Sikh people who wear turbans, have also been subjected to these attacks. These racist attacks include verbal and physical threats, assault, and murder (Iyer, 2015). Many victims of this type of targeting have been forced to perpetuate othering by ceasing to wear turbans or hijabs, cutting their hair, or other acts that parallel shunning their own cultures in an effort to appear more "Western." Because of the fear of racist attacks, Asian Indian and South Asian communities have also perpetuated discrimination against their own people who identify as Muslim. Anti-Muslim racism is not new to Asian Indian communities; even in India, people hold prejudices against Muslim communities due to historic and long-standing tensions.[2] However, the fear of racist attacks may maintain perpetuation of discrimination as a survival mechanism for non-Muslim Asian Indians in the United States.

Asian Indian individuals can also experience discrimination to varying degrees based on whether or not they have an accent. As discussed in the generational differences section, Asian Indians experience direct and indirect effects of immigration across generational statuses because their physical attributes (such as brown skin) make them identifiable as immigrants. However, people born in the United States and who have more flexible accents (or what is perceived in the United States as having no accent) may experience this discrimination in the form of curiosity (e.g., "Where are you from?" or "Where is your family from?"), whereas those with discernable accents may experience it more in the form of hateful or xenophobic othering (e.g., "Go back to your country").

The level of immediate danger, the physical or psychological nature, and the source (Western society or Asian Indian society) of discrimination can have varying effects on how a person reacts to their experience. Sometimes, Asian Indians may experience multiple types of discrimination at the same time, based on identities they hold. They may even experience the traumas of second- or third-hand discrimination. For example, a Sikh woman may struggle with second-hand effects of racist attacks against a male family member who wears a turban; at the same time, she may experience first-hand discrimination from Western society based on her accent and from Asian Indian society based on her dark complexion. These overlapping experiences and the heterogeneity of discrimination are important to note when considering how immigration, discrimination, and internalized racism function together to influence the identity development and mental health of Asian Indians in the United States.

Indian Caste System: The Rain

The intent of this section on caste is not to provide an extensive history of the oppressive roots of the Indian caste system but rather to present a basic framework for understanding how significantly the caste system affects Asian Indian people in the South Asian subcontinent and in the United States. It is not possible to provide a holistic framework of Asian Indians' experiences without mentioning how caste has shaped their experiences; to fail to provide such a framework would be akin to erasure of caste hierarchy and caste oppression. While acknowledging this, we also note that we write about the caste system as people who have benefited from the work of Dalit, Asian Indian indigenous, and caste-marginalized background pioneers and scholars in the field who have been writing about caste and caste genocide for a long time. In an attempt to highlight their work, we have cited and listed some recommended readings for in-depth history at the end of this chapter.

When Asian Indians immigrate to the United States, they navigate between differential systems of power and equity, othering, and discrimination. Hierarchical systems of power are not necessarily novel experiences for the Asian Indian population in the United States. India has its own system of oppression that bears resemblance to White supremacy, familiarizing Asian Indians with navigating inequitable societal infrastructure (Ambedkar, 1948; Wilkerson, 2020). However, an important context to consider when attempting to contextualize the influence of culture on the Asian Indian population is that while inequity is often a clear component of White supremacy, it is not often linked with caste. Equity refers to whether each person has access to opportunities, resources, and support needed to survive and thrive in a given society (Falk et al., 1993; Lee & Navarro, 2018). Equity models then have to take into consideration the analysis of fair distribution of both privileges and barriers which should be evidenced in impartial and equitable policies for everyone in a society (Falk et al., 1993; Lee & Navarro, 2018). What will become apparent as we delve deeper into our discussion of Asian Indian culture is that hierarchy permeates throughout it.

The Indian caste system originated from Brahmanism, the earliest form of the ancient religion known today as Hinduism. Caste has had widespread and significant influence on individuals of Asian Indian descent, and parallels the Eurocentric system of White supremacy in several ways (Ambedkar, 1948; Wilkerson, 2020). When Brahmanical ideologies are discussed, it is in reference to the ancient Hindu scriptures that are referred to as the **Vedas**, which dictate norms, guidelines, and rituals of Hindu culture and way of life. One of the largest cultural elements in these texts is the notion of a caste-based hierarchical system, in which the Vedas referred to castes as **varnas** (Kapoor, 2007).

While White supremacy (perpetuated by racism) and the Indian caste system are both institutionalized forms of hierarchical inequity that maintain power, privilege, and oppression of groups of people, the difference is that the caste system has no definable physical characteristics that are used to distinguish members of different castes (Falk et al., 1993). Caste and race, although different, are correlated concepts because they both are graded social categories used to distinguish groups of people, without individual and group freedom to move up in the system. Similar to racialized experiences in the United States, an individual's caste background determines whether an individual has equitable access to housing, employment, and educational opportunities as well as societal status, prestige, and esteem. Further, caste influences whether respect, humanity, and privileges are given or withheld as well as the access to resources based on the perceived rank of their caste or non-caste background (Falk et al., 1993). See Figure 1.1 for a visual of the caste system. In this sense, the parallelism between caste and race is that they inform who is considered "superior" and who is "inferior," dictating who gets to make decisions, has economic and political power, and has access to educational and economic resources.

A common understanding of the Indian caste system is based on definitions perpetuated by individuals of upper-caste status, which describes the Indian caste system as group differentiation based on occupational categorization. For the purposes of understanding the structure of the caste system, we will describe it here; however, it is important to note that this simplistic view of caste can be reductive of the extent of the marginalization that occurs because of this arbitrary hierarchy.

There are four castes (varnas) in the Indian caste system: Brahmins (priests), Kshatriya (warriors and royalty), Vaishya (farmers, landowners, and skilled trade workers), and Shudra (tenant farmers and servants) (Ambedkar, 1948;

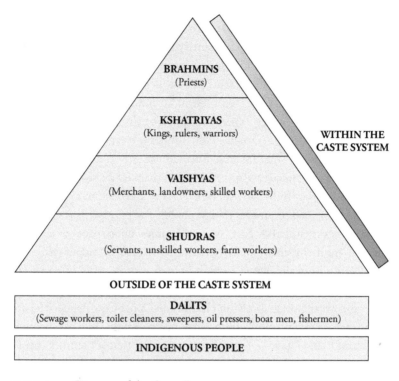

FIGURE 1.1   Diagram of the Caste System

Note: Many similar figures depicting the Indian caste structure exist in the current literature.

Falk et al., 1993; Wilkerson, 2020). Since the caste system is hierarchical, Brahmins are listed at the top, while the Shudras are listed at the bottom of this pyramid. An essential distinction to note is that while there are four groups recognized within the caste hierarchy, there are also several regional-based (e.g., northern, southern, western) subgroups within these categories (see *Annihilation of Caste*, Ambedkar, 1948, for a comprehensive overview of the Indian caste system). Although we provide a simplistic illustration of the caste system (defined via occupations), it is important to note that the caste system is interconnected with socioeconomic class, power, marriage, and politics (Kapoor, 2007). The system is founded on concepts of purity and impurity, hereditary occupations, and the accumulation of karma (good and bad deeds) from a previous life, which show up in cultural practices (Kapoor, 2007; Szczepanski, 2020).

Individuals are born into, work, marry, and die within their castes; as such, there is no social mobility within the caste system (Szczepanski, 2020). People born outside of the caste (varna) system are therefore considered casteless (avarna) and historically referred to as "untouchables." Today, members of this community may identify themselves as **Dalit** or **Harijan**, but politically these communities are now often referred to as individuals from "scheduled castes," illustrating the influence of caste even in today's society. "Respectable," "pure," and "clean" professions are associated with higher castes, while "dirty" and "impure" occupations such as cleaning sewages or latrines and removing cow dung are reserved for people born outside of the caste system (Szczepanski, 2020).

Outside of occupational categorization, untouchability is also deeply ingrained into the fabric of how Indian society differentiates and dehumanizes "casteless" or caste-oppressed communities (Singh, 2020). For example, caste-oppressed communities were not allowed to enter the same public spaces or services as those who are members of an assigned caste. Moreover, upper-caste Asian Indians have historically placed animals as higher in the order of purity (and, thus, respectability) than lower-caste and caste-oppressed communities (e.g., consider the worshipping of cows in Hinduism). Upper-caste people who came into physical contact with an untouchable person would think of themselves as dirty and then engage in a purification process that sometimes involved chanting prayers or sprinkling water on themselves to cleanse themselves of the untouchability (Kapoor, 2007). As you can see, the parallels with the American racial hierarchy and systemic racism become more apparent.

Dalit Panthers and Connection With Black Panthers

There is a common misperception that the Indian caste system was implemented during British colonial rule; however, while the British used the existing caste system as a means of social control, the caste system has been documented and traced back to 400 BCE (Szczepanski, 2020). The historical oppression of individuals who fall outside of the caste system has resulted in cultural genocide for centuries. The origins of why ancient Indian society decided to differentiate themselves in these ways is much contested, and different theories have originated as to how one's caste was determined, assigned, and passed on through generations (Ambedkar, 1948). For example, it is possible that groups of people who had varying cultural practices or religions (e.g., Buddhism or other Asian Indian indigenous religions) or resisted the hierarchical order were not afforded privileges of being included in the caste system or that the group of people who founded the caste system were not actually as indigenous to the continent as some other communities (Ambedkar, 1948).

Asian Indians belonging to caste-oppressed backgrounds renamed themselves "Dalit" in the 1930s. In Sanskrit or Hindi languages, Dalit translates to mean "broken" or "oppressed" and was used as a way for caste-oppressed individuals to reclaim their identity, and was also used as part of resistance and liberatory movements (Reddy, 2005). As discussed earlier, there are parallels between systems of White supremacy and the caste system. White supremacy has resulted in the global colonization of individuals from various racial and ethnic backgrounds, including individuals from India (and other countries within South Asia); one of the most insidious histories of oppression has been chattel slavery, colonization, and oppression of Black people (Reddy, 2005). Dalit communities resonated with the experiences of dehumanization and oppression of Black people, and as such were inspired by the ways in which the Black Panthers engaged in liberation and advocacy movements to dismantle systemic oppression of Black people in the United States (Reddy, 2005; Paul, 2018). The Dalit Panthers is a political advocacy organization that was founded by Namdeo Dhasal, Raja Dhale, and Arun Kamble in 1972 as a resistance movement to address caste-based genocide in India. The practice of caste segregation continues to maintain economic and social inequalities as well as physical violence and oppression of Dalit and indigenous communities in India and other countries in South Asia (Falk et al., 1993; Szczepanski, 2020; Singh, 2020).

One reason that casteism is able to persist today is because our society follows a capitalist structure. Capitalism enables the financing of the caste system, which allows upper-caste Asian Indians to maintain their status in Indian society. For example, Hindu temples often consist of an economic system that includes donations asked from devotees of temples to fund new temples and ceremonies (often graded by class: those who pay higher donations may have easier access to enter temples and engage in ceremonies while middle- or lower-class Asian Indians wait in long lines and have limited time to be in the temple) as well as payment for Brahmins (priests) to conduct prayer rituals for festivals, weddings, cleansing, or death ceremonies. Capitalism also involves right-wing Indian nationalists and high-ranking government officials who promote special ashrams that lure foreigners and tourists from different countries to pay high fees for spiritual awakenings or profound healing experiences. Such marketing allows for the exoticization of spiritual or religious practices, draws in more financial capital, and masks discriminatory practices. Many of these ashrams earn millions of dollars in revenue from the marketing and allowances of the Indian government.

Our acknowledgment of the influence of capitalism here is not to demean or diminish the healing benefits of such ashrams or places of worship where many Asian Indians have found peace, salvation, and healing. However, some of these ashrams have been found to exploit their devotees, especially women, foreigners, and those from marginalized communities.

Casteism Outside of Hinduism

Many Dalit communities began adopting other religions to escape the caste oppression that they experienced in Hinduism. Religions such as Sikhism were formed due to the rejection of central tenets of Hinduism involving the purity and impurity complex and as a way for individuals to be liberated from the caste system (Puri, 2003). Many Dalit and caste-oppressed communities also turned to other religions such as Buddhism, Islam, and Christianity to escape casteism. However, casteism began to seep into cultural practices within communities that practiced other religions, and as such, despite its scriptures and intent of escaping casteism, Sikhism too has what is called a Sikh caste hierarchy that bears resemblance to the Hindu caste system (Ali, 2002; Puri, 2003). As a coping mechanism to navigate and survive in society, marginalized communities tend to emulate the cultural practices of those in dominant positions; thus, it is unsurprising that caste-oppressed communities began to adopt the cultural practices (i.e., the caste system) of those of the dominant religion and culture (i.e., Hinduism). Thus, Asian Indians who practice other religions may still culturally practice casteism even if it is not formally sanctioned within their respective religions; this practice may look different due to the departure from Hindu caste/varna categories. For example, in some regions of India, Indian Muslims may use lineage to differentiate among themselves (e.g., "What is your last name?" or "What is your family name?"); however, unlike in Hindu-based caste practices, the caste hierarchy for Indian Muslims does not tend to affect cultural traditions or religious activities (Ali, 2002). Further, caste-based distinctions in the Indian Muslim community can be complex, as lineage differentiations can exist based on foreign (non-Indian) lineage or the caste background of individuals who converted to Islam (i.e., upper- or lower-caste Hindu converts) (Ahmad, 1978; Ali, 2002). While the cultural casteist practices in non-Hindu religious communities may not function in the exact manner as it does in Hindu communities, it can still manifest and influence decisions around hiring, conducting business, social relationships, and matrimonial alliances. While non-Hindu Dalit communities may not experience caste-based oppression as significantly as they do within

Hinduism, casteism still functions to maintain the disenfranchisement of these communities.

Modern-Day Caste System

While the caste system tends to be viewed in modern times as "obsolete," it still continues to affect the lives of millions of Asian Indian people in the Indian subcontinent (Singh, 2020). There is a common misperception that Asian Indians who immigrate to the United States are liberated from the caste system due to the United States having different dominant cultural practices and policies. However, Asian Indians in the United States simply experience caste that is refashioned to suit Asian Indian immigrant communities. Furthermore, history has shown that dominant frameworks are often the most promoted and publicized in the interest of protecting individuals who are privileged by the systems (Falk et al., 1993; Szczepanski, 2020). As a result, the caste system, like the system of White supremacy over the years, has modified and adapted to different times.

Asian Indian immigrants are not only assigned a racial minority status upon their arrival to the United States, but they also bring with them complicated experiences of power and privilege (e.g., if they are upper caste) or oppression (e.g., if they are Dalit-identified, lower caste, or Asian Indian indigenous and religious minorities). Within Asian Indian immigrant communities, those who identify as Dalit, indigenous, or lower caste may bring with them an added history of intergenerational trauma and oppression that may be exacerbated with the stress of immigration, racial and caste discrimination, and navigating a new dominant culture. For others, experiences of discrimination, exclusion, and marginalization may be new experiences after immigration to the United States due to their ancestry being part of dominant and privileged identities in India. Thus, recognition of cultural context is important due to its significant and complex influences on mental health and identity development of the Asian Indian population in the United States.

The caste system also manifests in a myriad of ways for the Asian Indian population residing in the United States (Paul, 2018). One might wonder how caste is determined if, unlike race, it is an invisible categorization. Asian Indians may discover an individual's caste background through lineage (last name), region (ancestral city, town, or village in India), matrimonial alliances, celebration of certain religious festivals, intergenerational occupational histories, social class, and ancestry. Many Asian Indians may use the caste system to identify themselves with those who belong to the same caste or village. The shared caste background may foster a sense of community for some Asian Indians. However, due to the nature of power and privilege in their native countries, people who are usually able to immigrate to the United States tend to be those who identify as upper caste, upper class, and Hindu. Thus, those who do not identify as Hindu are of lower caste or have lower socioeconomic status, or those who identify as Dalit may find themselves excluded from Asian Indian community organizations and events (Dube, 1996). Further, Asian Indians in the United States may take caste background into consideration for relationships and marriage partner decisions, and inter-Asian Indian solidarity in the workforce may also depend on one's caste background (*see Caste in the United States: A Survey of Caste Among South Asian Americans*, Zwick-Maitreyi et al., 2018). The manner in which the caste system is embedded within Asian Indian communities may also explain their separation from and accepted racism of other communities of color.[3]

Colorism

It can often be bewildering to attempt to comprehend how non-Black communities of color seemingly easily accept anti-Black racism in American society. However, if we consider the historical context of the Indian caste system in Asian Indian communities—a hierarchical system in which some lives are valued and humanized more than others—it is easier to see how the acceptance of another hierarchical system is not out of the ordinary. It might not even be a conscious process, but rather a generational societal conditioning that individuals accept because it is already inherent in their own cultural practices and traditions. The idea here is that living and practicing one hierarchical system of oppression makes it easier to adopt additional ones because the value structures are the same.

When multiple systems of oppression overlap like this, the methods by which the hierarchies are enforced also overlap. New hierarchical ideologies can emerge. At the intersection of caste and race is the practice of discrimination based on skin tone, known as **colorism**. Colorism is akin to but not quite the same as racism, in that rather than focusing on racial categorization—which can involve characteristics unrelated to skin color—the hierarchy is essentially based on the amount of melanin in the skin. It is, of course, used as a way to further perpetuate White supremacy since White people have lighter skin tones than People of Color; but it is also connected to social status in similar ways to caste. In Asian Indian culture, the association of lighter skin tones with higher societal status is grounded, in part, in the perception of certain occupations. Some types of occupations are viewed as being more prestigious than others—the more prestigious being those that involve less exposure to the sun because they include the luxury of staying indoors, and the less prestigious being those that involve manual labor in the sun. Thus, colorism is fueled by the idea that darker skin tones are related to more exposure to the sun, so people with darker skin tones must work less prestigious jobs and are therefore lower in the social hierarchy than those with lighter skin tones.

There are, of course, other factors that can be associated with an individual having a lighter skin tone, such as genetic factors and geographical region of residence (e.g., someone born and raised in the Southern regions of India versus northern regions of India). However, unlike race, skin tone is something that people can control a little bit; therefore, as a reaction to colorism, some people take active steps to attempt to lighten their skin tones by limiting exposure to the sun, using skin-whitening creams or remedies, or undergoing surgical procedures. Some people take steps to try to achieve the opposite effect on skin tone; for example, tanning is quite common in parts of the United States. However, people who tan are typically those who have the privilege of regularly having lighter skin—they are less likely to be discriminated against based on skin tone because they are perceived as light-skinned people participating in tanning for leisure. They have the luxury of acquiring a darker skin tone for a short period of time, without suffering the consequences of colorism. This is how colorism perpetuates White supremacy: people with naturally darker skin tones suffer discrimination based on colorism, while their skin tones are aestheticized and experienced in a temporary way, without consequence, by people who have light-skin privilege.

Outside of occupational and societal status, individuals with lighter skin tones often tend to be viewed as being more attractive and intelligent, and in this way more worthy of love, support, or respect than those with darker skin tones. Thus, the color of someone's skin influences familial and romantic relationships, self-perception, and career aspirations. In Asian Indian culture, the impact of colorism is also influenced by a person's gender (or perceived gender). Where the gender binary is enforced, Asian Indian women are expected to embody certain characteristics in order to fulfill one of their primary gender role expectations: to receive viable marriage prospects. As lighter skin is viewed as more desirable, having a darker skin tone could complicate finding romantic or marital partners. Because colorism is ingrained in Asian Indian culture, it can impact the experiences and overall mental health of Asian Indians in multiple ways, particularly based on the full constellation of identities they hold. We encourage you to think about how and why colorism and discrimination might look differently for people—even within the Asian Indian diaspora.

Patriarchy: The Torrential Wind

Asian Indian communities inherently operate within their family systems and communities through **collectivistic** cultural frameworks (Chadda & Deb, 2013). Collectivistic cultures value family cohesion and connection, cooperation, shared decision-making, interdependence, deference to elders, and conformity (Chadda & Deb, 2013). Historically, it was common for Asian Indians to reside in **joint families**, which refers to three or four generations (including great-grandparents, grandparents, uncles, aunts, and cousins) who live in the same residence (Chadda & Deb, 2013; Das & Kemp, 1997; Segal, 1991). Residing in joint families allowed for the development of stable, close, and enduring relationships with more than just immediate family members. Joint families also tended to share financial, caretaking, and household division responsibilities, which allowed for less burden to be placed on just one or two family members. In these types of family structures, household decision-making, values, and traditions were taken for the benefit of the family as a whole rather than as individual choices (Segal, 1991, 1998). It is worth mentioning that the joint family structure was not universally common for Asian Indians, as families from lower socioeconomic status or lower-caste backgrounds did not often have the financial means to support larger family structures (Caldwell et al., 1984; Chakravorty et al., 2021). There are fewer joint families in India today due to a myriad of reasons, including the changing sociodemographic landscapes and increased urbanization and industrialization. Regardless of whether Asian Indians reside in joint or nuclear families, living in the same country or state allows for easier access to family support networks.

In contrast, Asian Indians who immigrate to the United States tend to reside with just their nuclear family (i.e., their spouse and children) because immigration is not always possible for entire joint families. Asian Indian immigrants who have families already living in the United States will often reside with them until they are financially able to afford living on their own. Collectivistic cultural norms are valuable in both types of family living situations because it can be common for family members to be relied on for providing childcare assistance if both parents are employed.

Another strength of collectivistic values emerges in the form of strong Asian Indian networks that can help newly arrived Asian Indian immigrants to navigate their new city and its culture better than they would on their own. Collectivistic cultural values—which diverge from Eurocentric values that traditionally emphasize individualism, autonomous decision-making, and personal achievement—can buffer against the stress of immigration and alleviate experiences of alienation that Asian Indian immigrants may feel. A collectivist orientation toward community can also aid Asian Indian immigrants in maintaining relationships with their families and communities within and outside of the United States.

Patriarchy and Hierarchical Decision-Making

As described above, collectivistic values have historically shaped the structure of Asian Indian families. While collectivistic values can offer several benefits and protective factors for Asian Indian Americans, inherent in this value system is also the influence of heteropatriarchy, which often perpetuates gender-based inequalities. Patriarchy is an ancient system that is very deeply ingrained in how Asian Indian culture delineates and assigns normative value to gender, power, and relationships. Patriarchy references "the father" or "the patriarch," and male power and dominance over other genders and marginalized communities; it is much more than power over any one individual because it represents a much larger system (Bhasin, 1993; Walby, 1990). Asian Indian norms of patriarchy often intertwine with that of Western patriarchy with some similarities and differences. It is important to note that our discussion of patriarchy here references the larger system of oppression rather than a specific familial structure, as patriarchal oppression can be present also in matriarchal families and in families where there are no men.

Asian Indian forms of patriarchy differ from Western systems of patriarchy with its strong focus on hierarchical decision-making structures in families. While male figures typically assume leadership with regards to decision-making roles in the household, this norm is also dependent on who the eldest family member is in the home. In the United States, depending on whether an Asian Indian family is residing in a nuclear (parents and siblings) or joint family dynamic, emphasis is placed on respecting, honoring, and caring for elders in the family, which also means deference to the eldest members of the family for making major life decisions. These kinds of important life decisions or lifestyle choices can include career aspirations, employment decisions, living situations, dating choices, or marriage partners. Traditionally, decision-making norms were structured in this hierarchical manner because of the notion that older family members have more life experience and knowledge that can help guide their younger generations. However, patriarchal norms can provide women (here we refer to cisgender women specifically) in these families with differential power where they have more or less power depending on the context (Chakravorty et al., 2021). For example, younger Asian Indian women often have decisions made for them that they may not necessarily have chosen for themselves: their families may select a marriage partner for them, impose what attire is appropriate for women to wear, have financial restrictions, or dictate which characteristics are appropriate versus inappropriate for women to have. However, older Asian Indian women may hold more power over younger male family members. This gendered division can also extend to religious places of worship whereby men and women are seated separately (sometimes all the men sit in the front while women sit at the back), and men lead processions or rituals and are served meals first. As clinicians, we can sometimes have a monolithic approach when we learn of parallel systems of inequality across cultures, but this type of approach often invisibilizes the unique and nuanced differences that individuals experience. Taking these nuances a step further, consider how patriarchy and feminism may be experienced differently for Asian Indian women than for White women, for Asian Indian upper-caste women than for Dalit women, or for Asian Indian Muslim women than for Asian Indian Sikh women.

Asian Indian families residing in the United States may experience varying degrees of shifts in their family structures, decision-making processes, and complexities within their relationships as a consequence of differential levels of cultural adaptation processes when they immigrate to the United States. While older generations may have more life experience and wisdom related to relationships, cultural norms, and values, younger generations tend to be more knowledgeable and familiar with dominant cultural norms in the United States. Thus, younger generations may provide guidance to older family members by translating American English (if English fluency is limited), completing paperwork, navigating procedures, or explaining American cultural norms. This duality of roles, whereby younger generations must seek approval and obtain guidance about major life decisions from their older family members and yet also hold the responsibility of guiding and helping with the adjustment of their older family members, can make family relationships quite complicated. Older family members who struggle with adjusting to American culture and systems may experience and internalize shame for needing to rely on their younger family members for guidance.

These relationships are further complicated with the divergent levels of cultural shifts that may be occurring with younger generations of Asian Indians. Asian Indians across generational statuses tend to practice both their heritage (Asian Indian) and dominant cultures in different ways, which often gives rise to bicultural identity conflicts within families. For example, younger generations tend to adopt mainstream American cultural norms more so than their elder family members, which can negatively impact relationships because it is perceived as a departure from or rejection of heritage culture. The easier adoption of American mainstream cultural values by younger generations of Asian Indian descent produces what is referred to as bicultural identity clashes, as a result of the conflict between striving for independence in **individualistic** cultures and family-oriented collectivistic values. Because the family is prioritized over the self in collectivist cultures, personal needs and space are more interconnected for people who practice collectivism. For others, this other-over-self-prioritization may be experienced as a neglect of personal needs and space.

Communication and relationship difficulties related to patriarchal family structure can cultivate an environment in which it is possible to pass on intergenerational trauma. Trauma (e.g., as a result of systems of oppression) when it is left unhealed can become integrated into relational patterns between generations. The trauma is then learned, integrated, and compounded in the lives of each subsequent generation, which ultimately presents barriers for the healing of these ancestral wounds.

Binary Gender Norms

While there are clear benefits to the hierarchical decision-making process involving deference to elders for guidance, we have described how this may also reinforce patriarchal archetypes and deny identities or experiences that vary from heteronormativity. Similar to gender roles in Western cultures, gender roles in Asian Indian culture typically follow patriarchal systems, though they may be more explicit and hierarchical in nature. As a result, male figures tend to have increased autonomy and adopt the role of final decision-makers within family systems, while female-identifying individuals are taught from childhood to abide with male-identified family members and spouses.

Asian Indians residing in the United States may embrace more egalitarian roles with regard to household division and careers. The challenges associated with immigration may require both partners to be employed and striving to establish their careers at the same time; however, patriarchal-gendered expectations still exist in these relationships as well. For example, Asian Indian women may be held to stricter norms around relationships and sex than Asian Indian males, where there is an expectation of females to abstain from sexual intercourse, to have limited sexual experience, or to not have had multiple previous romantic partners. Due to the evolving nature of relationship dynamics in this community, expectations may vary across generations and age whereby American-born, young immigrants, or recently immigrated Asian Indian youth or young adults, may have more liberal and equitable attitudes around sex across gender roles. Another way that patriarchal-gendered expectations may show up even within outwardly egalitarian relationships is the expectation that the female partner will adjust her life—move to the same city or state as her partner, change jobs to accommodate partnership, or have higher expectations of compromise and adjustments in romantic partnerships.

Third Gender Paradox

Even though Asian Indian society has historically reflected patriarchal and binary gender norms, India has recognized a third gender for a very long time. Frequently, from a Western perspective, this is considered to be somewhat radical or progressive; at face value, recognition of a third gender appears to directly contradict otherwise oppressive systems of patriarchy that are prevalent across borders, even in Western societies. *Third gender* can sometimes be synonymous with Asian Indian people who identify as **Hijra** (eunuchs) but not all members of the community prefer this term due to it also being used as slurs against the community. Individuals who identify as Hijra are traditionally male-bodied, feminine-identified people, but the community itself can encompass individuals who are intersex, cross dressers, transexual, transvestite, and hermaphrodite (Hossain, 2017). Asian Indians who do not identify within the gender binary system or heterosexual identity may also use "third gender" to identify themselves.

Historically, Hijra have been perceived as people who give up their male genitalia in order to receive spiritual power to bless and/or curse newly wedded couples or newborn infants (Nanda, 1999). The existence of Hijra people in Indian society can be traced back centuries as reflected in Hindu scriptures, texts, and mythology; Hijra people had administrative positions in royal courts during the Mughal era, and their histories can also be traced within Indigenous Indian histories in India (Nambiar, 2017). Hijra people are viewed as individuals with tremendous spiritual power and as such are sought for blessings during religious ceremonies (Nambiar, 2017). Historical narratives have shown that attitudes about Hijra and nonbinary gender communities have changed since British colonization in India, which brought more "puritan" ideas of what sexuality and gender should look like and attempted to criminalize the Hijra community via laws (Nambiar, 2017). The current laws in India extend to legal identification as "third gender," and certain states have centers where individuals can get a sex reassignment surgery; however, the effects of British colonization have left deep imprints that have marginalized the Hijra community in significant ways (Mancino, 2019).

Although Asian Indians have in some ways politically and culturally recognized the existence of a third gender (nonbinary gender), the recognition has not always translated into widespread societal acceptance and inclusion. In other words, Asian Indian society has often been paradoxical in its legal acceptance yet subsequent societal rejection of third gender or nonbinary Asian Indians. Historically, those who identify as Hijra or **Kinnar** were cast out of their homes and resided in reclusive multi-faith Kinnar communities due to family and community rejection. At other times, the tradition of the Hijra and Kinnar communities has been to seek out other Hijra or Kinnar people still residing with their families to encourage them to leave their homes in favor of Hijra community spaces as a preemptive measure in anticipation of rejection or persecution. The Hijra community then becomes their chosen family and people often no longer have contact with their biological family or other community members (Mancino, 2019).

Sometimes, Hijra and Kinnar communities are invited to (or crash) weddings to bless a newly wedded couple, or attend baby showers or homes with newborns to bless the child. In return, they receive some monetary gifts for their blessings. Outside of this kind of "acceptance," Hijra communities are often mocked, assaulted, or forced into sex work. In addition to the complex and paradoxical nature of their experiences, the marginalization of the Hijra community also often leads to the erasure of how it maintains community and resiliency despite the continued oppression within Asian Indian dominant cultural spaces. Recall our previous discussion of how shared experiences of oppression and resilience can be integral for the formation of community and identity: it is important to acknowledge the strength, such as one's chosen family.

The treatment and conceptualization of third-gender people transcend into the identity development of Asian Indians who immigrate to the United States due to the inherent binary-gendered, patriarchal frameworks embedded within Asian Indian culture. A child who does not identify within these binary gender norms can experience significant risk with regard to disclosing their nonbinary gender identity to their parents. In mainstream Western culture, rejection associated with identifying as transgender or nonbinary may mean rejection from families and friends who do not accept these gender identities. However, Asian Indians who identify outside of the gender binary may experience two layers of rejection. The first layer occurs as a result of the lack of recognition and acceptance of their gender identity from parents and families. The second is racial and ethnic marginalization they may experience within Eurocentric transgender or nonbinary communities[4] and the loss of community they may have found in India with other Hijra and nonbinary individuals.

Dating and Marriage: Heteronormativity and Patriarchy

Thus far, we have described how the resemblance in systems of oppression between Asian Indian and Western culture—such as White supremacy and the caste system—can amplify challenges and mental health concerns for Asian Indians who live in the United States. These parallels and subsequent challenges are also prevalent in the ways in which dating and marriage are practiced and endorsed within the culture.

Traditionally, marriages within Asian Indian culture are arranged, which means that relatives select the partner for a person who is ready to get married. Within the collectivistic cultural norm of deferring to the wisdom of elders for decision-making due to their life experience, authority in choosing a partner is given to parents and families, as they are perceived to have the most knowledge in determining which suitors would be a good fit for their children and families. Traditional (historical) arranged marriages often occur without each partner meeting in person or communicating with each other prior to the marriage. In certain religions such as Islam, dating, premarital sex, and cohabitation are prohibited prior to marriage, which reinforces the arranged marriage ideal (Zaidi & Shuraydi, 2002). In Asian Indian communities, marriages are not just between two individuals but between two families, which is why they tend to consider whether a potential marriage suitor is not only a good partner for their children but also a match for their families (Zaidi & Shuraydi, 2002). Thus, people who desire arranged marriages believe that their family's perspective is valuable in making a sound decision about the best match for them.

In a more modernized arranged marriage dynamic, an individual is presented with what is called a **biodata**, which comprises a potential suitor's name, parents' names, location, caste, religion, education and career information, personal interests, and physical characteristics (e.g., skin color, height, weight, and health concerns). The biodata also includes photographs of the potential partner. Sometimes biodatas are received from a matchmaker that the family is consulting with or hired for the purpose of finding a marital alliance. Based on this information, families may decide to move forward and discuss a potential marriage alliance between their children. Families assess whether they mesh with one another, while the potential couples also meet as individuals. Some individuals may decide to meet with their potential partners in person, either on their own or chaperoned by their parents or other family members, and may make a decision about whether to get married after a few brief in-person meetings. In contrast to Western forms of dating, there is often no physical or sexual contact between potential partners prior to an arranged marriage.

While many Asian Indians still practice arranged marriages in India and abroad, there is more variability today in how they might pursue romantic relationships and marriages. Some Asian Indians may find partners on their own by dating through in-person encounters, family or community networks, Indian matrimonial conventions, matchmakers, or dating websites (mainstream dating and South Asian matrimonial sites). Some Asian Indian parents may travel to find a potential partner for their adult children. Regardless of the route taken to pursue long-term relationships or marriages, decisions will still typically consider whether family members approve of the relationship and whether both partners' families will get along with one another. It should be noted that this discussion of dating and marriage operates within the heteronormative framework and can contribute to the erasure of identities that fall beyond the heterosexual partnership.

Land of Kamasutra: Sexual Liberation Versus Sexual Control

A further illustration of the nuances and complexities within Asian Indian culture is that sex can also be explained as a paradoxical concept in Asian Indian communities. The Kamasutra is an ancient Sanskrit text that originated in India and is known for its discussion on eroticism, sexuality, relationships, and sexual pleasures (which entails details on different sex positions and emotional fulfillment). This can be bewildering to some, because India and Asian Indians are often perceived as "sexually repressive." Somewhere along the course of history, Asian Indian attitudes toward sex and sexuality evolved to more puritan and repressive perspectives, despite the existence of ancient texts and teachings such as the Kamasutra, paintings, and other scriptures that showcase more sexual liberatory perspectives. Consequently, talking about or insinuating sex, sexual pleasure, or related experiences such as dating or showing emotional or physical affection might be uncomfortable for Asian Indians and their families.

As a result, Asian Indians tend to have a strong sense of negativity or avoidance around sex, yet they often subsequently perpetuate heteronormative expectations around wanting their married children to have kids, following collectivistic values of procreation, and creating and participating in community. It is not uncommon for Asian Indian parents to restrict any sexually explicit content (even if it is PG13 material) even for their 17- or 18-year-old children. This differs from Western communities in the sense that while there may be reluctance with talking about sex or sexuality with parents or other family members, there is a level of openness in discussing romantic relationships or to bringing dates to family gatherings. Further, there is even more openness to conversing about these topics among peers. In contrast, even among Asian Indian youth and young adults, there may be some discomfort and anxiety around discussing sex, masturbation, or sexuality in these settings. Asian Indians may also become sexually active at later ages than their non-Asian Indian peers, but paradoxically experience societal pressure to get married at similar or younger ages compared to their non-Asian Indian peers. For some Asian Indians, due to religious reasons (e.g., Asian Indians practicing Islam or Christianity), sexual intercourse or sexual acts do not occur between partners until after marriage.

As with dating and marriage, notions around sex and sexuality have begun to evolve for Asian Indian youth and young adults in the United States; as a result, Asian Indians may have varying levels of comfort and discomfort around sex and exploring their sexualities. Since most Asian Indian parents and Asian Indian elders tend to endorse stricter norms around sexual inhibitions (e.g., no sex prior to marriage, no multiple sexual partners), this may conflict with the experiences of their children, who may feel increased sexual liberation. The deep-rooted discomfort around sex in Asian Indian culture transcends into how sexuality and sexual orientation is viewed within communities. Similar to Western communities but also rooted in their own culture, it may be difficult for Asian Indians within a heteronormative framework to understand that sexuality and sexual orientation can be experienced differently.

Through an Asian Indian cultural lens, controlling sex can also be viewed as a method to maintain caste boundaries, given how caste is intrinsically based on the distinctions between "pure" (virginal) and "impure" (nonvirginal). The caste infrastructure is founded on the concept of **endogamy**, which culturally predisposes Asian Indians to pursue heterosexual within-caste partnerships.

In this sense, heteronormativity permeates throughout the caste system (both by those within and outside caste boundaries) as well as by those who practice religions other than Hinduism (Kumar, 2008; 2009).

Quite often when we attempt to dismantle stereotypical sexual roles and relationships through feminist pedagogies, discussions are limited to heterosexual partnerships (Mankekar, 2004; Menon, 2007). This can contribute to the erasure of relationships beyond the heterosexual binary (Mankekar, 2004; Menon, 2007), and it is therefore important to focus a discussion about mental health and identity development influences for those who identify outside of dominant gender and sexual frameworks.

Asian Indian Queer Communities

Due to the inherent heteronormative framework within Asian Indian communities, Asian Indians who identify outside of its confines can find it challenging to gain acceptance of their identities within their families and communities. We use *queer* to describe Asian Indian LGBTQIA+ communities (due to the lack of a singular and pure indigenous term that encompasses multiple identities); however, it is important to note that Asian Indians may use different indigenous terms to identify themselves depending on their immigration histories and cultural proximity. Queer is sometimes used as an umbrella term to include identities that are not captured with one singular term and is more inclusive for individuals who do not feel represented within larger LGBTQIA+ spaces, and for some, is a political identity to reject and destabilize heteronormativity (Kumar, 2008; 2009). With regard to nonbinary gender identities, Asian Indians within this community may identify as transgender, third gender, or may use indigenous terms such as Hijra, Kinnar, Zenana, Kothi, and Panthis (Gairola, 2017; Kumar, 2008; 2009). With regard to minority sexual orientation identities, Asian Indians may use lesbian, gay, bisexual, asexual, or queer (among others) to identify their sexual orientation or use regional-based identities such as *jogappa* and *jogtas* in northern Karnataka and Maharashtra or the *Shivshaktis* and *Ganacharis* in parts of Southern India (Kumar, 2008; 2009).

It is also important to become familiar with some of the history that has influenced and maintained the deep stigma of queer communities in India in order to contextualize Asian Indian queer experiences in the United States. India has an extensive history of the criminalization of queer communities. The Indian law system had what was called the Section 377 Indian Penal Code, which was implemented during the British colonial rule in 1861 (similar laws were drafted by the British in other South Asian countries) (Ahuja, 2017;

Gupta, 2005, 2006). Section 377 criminalized same-sex relationships as well as anal and oral sex in public and private spaces, which was illegal and punishable by law (Ejaz & Moscowitz, 2020). Indigenous histories across the world have alluded that sexual diversity has always been the norm and not the exception, which is also true for individuals in the Indian subcontinent. However, this law perpetuated paradoxical regressions in attitudes and perceptions around sex and sexuality, as discussed earlier (Ejaz & Moscowitz, 2020). Section 377 was recently challenged and abolished by the Indian Supreme Court in 2018, which was a significant victory for Asian Indian queer communities in India. However, the decriminalization did not translate to depathologization of same-sex relationships, and as a result, the majority of the Asian Indian queer population still remains hidden due to the fear of being harassed, persecuted, raped, or murdered (Ejaz & Moscowitz, 2020). The stigma and risk are so heightened for Asian Indian queer communities that even prominent and well-known personalities may not feel safe to disclose their sexual orientation or gender identities. The relative recency of the abolishment of this law illustrates the differences between the legal and societal acceptance of same sex relationships between India and the United States. It has been only six years since the landmark case *Obergefell v. Hodges* (2015) that legalized same sex marriages in all 50 states in the United States (though some states legalized same sex marriages prior to this case), but India has yet to establish legal acceptance of same-sex marriages.

This historical context of India's and surrounding South Asian countries' legal and sociocultural perceptions of queer identities is important to consider when understanding how these issues might manifest for Asian Indians residing in the United States. Due to the fairly recent decriminalization of same sex relationships, stigmatizing and heterosexist perspectives about sexuality and sexual orientation may still be prevalent for Asian Indian immigrants. Asian Indian queer individuals may thus be told they were "led astray," are "learning Western ways," that they "need to be a good child," and/or "need to choose to be in a heterosexual relationship." Some Asian Indians may also believe, based on religious beliefs or scriptures, that being queer is a sin.

Asian Indian parents may perceive their child's queer identity to be a result of their own "bad parenting." This may lead to the perpetuation of internal and external shaming and guilt within family systems. Asian Indian individuals with a queer identity may experience significant difficulties with receiving acceptance from their family members, and some may never receive it at all. Thus, they may choose to either disclose their sexual orientation or introduce their partners to their families much later in life than they otherwise would, or they may never share this with their families or communities. Further, Asian Indians may not resonate with Western ways of "coming out," revealing nonbinary gender identities or nonheterosexual sexual identities, because they may experience more complicated layers or consequences of their queer identities.

There is often a tendency for Asian Indians to perceive and treat queerness as an intangible Western concept, despite the existence of ancient scriptures and teachings that suggest that perceptions were not always this way in India (Azad & Nayak, 2016). This separation of queerness from Indianness—or implying that to be Indian means not to be queer, and asking their children to choose to be "good" representations of Indian children by rejecting queerness—then allows them to maintain what they see as "normal" and "acceptable." Thus, they distance themselves from what they do not understand or accept by ascribing it to Westernization and their Asian Indian culture becomes their safety net. As mentioned in previous sections about othering, this type of separation as a response to perceived "badness" can influence people in a myriad of ways, including their ability to find acceptance, community, and connection.

There may also be nuances with how queerness is seen and experienced within the Asian Indian community. Through an Asian Indian heteronormative lens, queerness is often perceived as synonymous with "maleness" while "femaleness" is linked with being heterosexual (Gopinath, 2005). This demonstrates how feminist and queer movements diverge from Western movements. Asian Indian queer depictions in the media, books, or movies tend to reinforce who is considered queer and who is not (Gopinath, 2005). Thus, Asian Indians who identify as female and queer may not be truly "seen" within the community and experience double rejection both within Asian Indian queer spaces and outside of it (Gopinath, 2005). Another often invisibilized group within the Asian Indian queer community is that of Dalit or lower-caste individuals. More often than not, these identities are invisibilized because queer movements in India tend to be by and for Asian Indians in metropolitan cities, who tend to have privileges through caste and class that allows for a better (albeit still miniscule) safety net compared to those from caste-marginalized backgrounds (Kumar, 2008; 2009; Ejaz & Moscowitz, 2020). Further, Asian Indian queer communities may experience marginalization and invisibility within larger, more Eurocentric LGBTQIA+ spaces in the United States—for reasons discussed, as well as because the cultural roots, including names and indigenous terms for how they identify, may not be acknowledged in these spaces. Thus, Asian Indian queer individuals experience complicated layers of trauma and rejection both within and outside of Asian Indian communities.

Intersectionality

What Is Intersectionality?

People who experience multiple overlapping systems of oppression, as discussed throughout this chapter, often have multiple identities that all carry varying levels of privilege and marginalization. Intersectionality describes the unique experience of discrimination stemming from the overlap, or *intersection*, of these different identities. The term was originally coined in 1989 by Kimberlé Crenshaw, a Black feminist scholar, to describe the unique ways in which Black women experienced discrimination in the workforce. Crenshaw highlighted how antiracist policies addressed the disparities between White and Black people, and feminist theory addressed disparities between men and women; however, neither of these movements focused on the dual overlapping marginalization experienced by individuals who identified both as Black and as women (Crenshaw, 1989). Black women do not experience discrimination in the same ways as White women because of the additional impact of racism; they also do not experience racism in the same ways as Black men because of the additional impact of sexism. Being at the intersection of the foci of both the antiracist and feminist movements meant that Black women were in the blind spots of these movements, and they essentially fell through the cracks. Thus, the introduction of intersectionality was important in highlighting these blind spots.

Our description of "the storm" is a metaphor for intersectionality. Dealing with differential impacts of multiple systems of oppression can create discomfort for individuals who must then navigate different levels of oppression under some systems and privilege under others. For example, consider our discussions of the parallels between racism, a Western system of oppression, and casteism, an Asian Indian system of oppression. Asian Indians in the United States who have a higher caste status may experience the intersection of these systems of oppression differently, where they are marginalized based on race but privileged based on caste.

Intersectionality can also describe individual characteristic-level discrimination in that specific identities that are marginalized across cultures may be marginalized in different ways. Individuals who live within both cultures then experience the overlap of the unique ways that identity is marginalized in both cultures at once. For example, gender minorities (e.g., nonbinary, gender nonconforming, and queer individuals) experience discrimination in both Asian Indian and Western cultures, but the discrimination has varying characteristics: in India, third-gender and other gender minorities are formally and legally recognized in ways that they are not in the United States. Thus, it is vital to think about the unique ways in which the intersection between these identities and being Asian Indian may impact Asian Indians in the United States.

Some Dimensions of Identity to Think About

It is beyond the scope of this book to describe and discuss every possible identity and intersectional "configuration" for Asian Indian individuals in the United States. To pay homage to the diversity in this population, some identity variables to keep in mind may include religion and religiosity, socioeconomic status, English language proficiency or multilingualism, education level, age, generational status, regional background in India, and more. Diversity may also include the saliency of these identities—that is, how important they are and how often individuals think about them. Further, experiences may be different for people who hold more than one racial identity, such as multiracial Asian Indian individuals. Ultimately, it is impossible to define what identity development and mental health looks like for Asian Indians in the United States; what we can do is paint a picture highlighting important aspects of shared identity and acknowledging the existence of diversity.

Mental Health: A History

We opened this chapter with an illustration of the hardships and resilience involved in living at the crux of three influential systems: racism, casteism, and patriarchy. While understanding hardships and resilience is a good start to begin conceptualizing the psychological impact of what we have called "the storm," we must also recognize the vagueness of these terms, and recognize that sometimes the storm has more specific and detrimental mental health implications. The subsequent chapters will provide further details about what these can look like; however, it is important to know that mental health implications for Asian Indians do not always fit squarely into Western frameworks of psychology. Here, we review briefly the historical background regarding Western psychology and why multicultural areas of study, such as ours, emerged. This information highlights the gap in the

Western understanding of mental health as well as the need for expanded and liberated frameworks, both of which we hope will help you to expand your thinking about mental health as you move through the rest of this book.

Historically, the study of psychology was grounded in the experiences of educated, White, cisgender male individuals living in Western or Eurocentric societies. Their experiences became known as the baseline that defined psychological health, and for the most part, people who did not meet the definition were considered to be mentally unwell or otherwise inferior to the normative population (Galton, 1883; Brigham, 1922). As you can imagine, not everyone's lived experience parallels that of Eurocentrically socialized, educated, White, cisgender men; thus, subfields of study emerged that explored differences in human experiences by highlighting identity variables in contrast to these demographics. For example, feminist psychology began as a critique of male-dominated psychological research and a claim that sociocultural experiences related to gender identity are important considerations in understanding and defining mental health in a way that is inclusive—rather than harmful—to women (Horney, 1993).[5]

Common understanding of what it looks like to be psychologically unwell is also based on the field's historic focus on a limited and defined majority population. For example, many psychological assessments used in both research and clinical practice were validated and normed on majority White participants. Therefore, the questions that are asked tend to be tailored to White experiences—or, perhaps more importantly, questions that are *not* asked may miss aspects of psychological well-being or illness that are meaningful for non-White populations. Compared to when psychology first developed as a field of study, reports of the importance of assessing somatic experiences such as headaches and stomachaches as reflections of mental health problems for People of Color are relatively recent, and again emerged as a response to the importance of acknowledging differences in experience based on identity (Mallinson & Popay, 2007; Rose & Cheung, 2012; Lara-Cinisomo et al., 2020). Asking the right questions is also extremely important in psychotherapy settings for successful therapeutic work, such as case conceptualization and treatment. It shows that clinicians are knowledgeable about how clients may be experiencing problems and illustrates the appropriateness of therapy for healing. Statistics on mental health service utilization have historically demonstrated that racial and ethnic minority communities tend to use mental health services less than White communities (Pescolido & Boyer, 1999; Soorkia et al., 2011; Kim & Zane, 2016). Given that psychology has been primarily informed through Eurocentric frameworks, our understanding of working with diverse communities may be limited. Thus, it is now our responsibility as clinicians to utilize our knowledge of the problematic history of our field to continue our trajectory toward developing and offering more multiculturally appropriate services.

Stigma: What Will People Say?

As mentioned previously, Asian Indians as a community are shaped by collectivistic cultural norms that value preserving and maintaining community, collective decision-making, and harmony in relationships. An additional layer to these values is the notion of "saving face," which refers to how one is perceived by society. How an individual presents to society often entails the level of status (i.e., determined through class, caste, and occupational choices), respect, and honor an individual and family is perceived to have; hence, attributes or situations that indicate they may "lose face" incite fear. When one member of an Asian Indian family is perceived as "dishonoring" the family, the entire family experiences the effects of it, which illustrates how collectivistic cultures operate.

As we consider the U.S. cultural context, there is also a clear nexus to the model minority framework, as Asian Indians perceive having a mental illness as indicative of failure and inability to fulfill the ideal of being a "successful minority immigrant" (Tummala-Narra et al., 2016). Thus, Asian Indian families who have ingrained this schema about what constitutes "acceptable" attributes of an Asian Indian person, whether it is the types of relationships, sexual orientation, gender roles, lifestyle choices (e.g., deciding not to marry or have children, divorced), or family systems, may perceive their family members who deviate from this schema as indicative of them "losing face" in society. The fear of "losing face" also intertwines with the deep stigma associated with mental illnesses in the Asian Indian community. Asian Indians may experience shame and perceive having a mental illness as a failure to cope with life's challenges, and as bringing dishonor to their families (Das & Kemp, 1997; Leung et al., 2011; Segal, 1991; Sue, 1994). Quite often, Asian Indians who are parents of children who have mental illnesses may perceive this as a failure of their parenting or that their child is not "praying enough," or was influenced by "bad" friends or "not working hard enough" to overcome their mental health challenges. As a way to cope and maintain these values, Asian Indians adopt silence and secrecy around mental illness (Sue & Morishima, 1982). Thus, it is common for Asian Indians to make significant efforts to hide that their family member has a mental illness even if the person would like to share this with others.

Mental illnesses are also often viewed as Western concepts, separate from Indianness, that do not affect Asian Indian communities. Associating mental illnesses as "Western concepts" allows for Asian Indians to not experience the shame and dishonor linked with having a mental illness and in this way, preserve the "honor" that they feel they would lose if they have a mental illness (Sue & Morishima, 1982).[6] However, as a result, many Asian Indians often experience significant isolation due to the adoption of silence in their families. Stigmatized beliefs about mental illnesses contribute not only to the low utilization rates of mental health services but also to the lack of recognition and acknowledgement of mental illnesses in the Asian Indian community (Bhatia et al., 1987; Malhotra et al., 1981; Segal, 1991). As a result, some Asian Indians may prefer to seek guidance from elders in the family or from religious gurus, or **fakirs**, instead of meeting with a cultural outsider (e.g., mental health professional) to discuss personal and familial challenges. These guides might recommend prayer or spirituality, **homeopathy** or **naturopathy**, meditation, amulets to ward off the **evil eye**, and other traditional healing practices (see Chapter 5).

Stigma often contributes to Asian Indians having low utilization rates of mental health services. Given this cultural context and lack of spaces to talk about mental health challenges, Asian Indian clients who do present to therapy may feel overwhelmed with how to express their mental health concerns. Thus, Asian Indian clients may not always provide a clear objective or reason for seeking therapy, or may express ambivalence about therapy, focus on somatic symptoms, as physical ailments are easier to describe, or present with difficulties related to a life goal (e.g., career, job, marriage, children). Further, Asian Indian clients may not return if they perceive their therapist to not operate from a culturally informed framework or if they feel like they have to explain or justify their culture. Bicultural navigation is a complex experience with multiple systems of inequality impacting an individual's experiences, which can exacerbate mental health in the Asian Indian population in the United States (Durvasula & Mylvaganam, 1994). Thus, the aim of this book is to help clinicians and clinicians-in-training gain a better understanding when working with this population and to learn some approaches that can aid in the treatment.

Figure Credit

Fig. 1.1: Adapted from Maari Zwick-Maitreyi, et al., *Caste in the United States: A Survey of Caste among South Asian Americans*, p. 9. Copyright © 2018 by Equality Labs.

Case Descriptions

Introduction

In Chapter 1, we posited that though Asian Indian identity development can be conceptualized through the framework of three important "pillars," we must also remain cognizant of the heterogeneity of this population and of intersectionality across identity variables (e.g., immigration, generational status, age, caste identity, gender identity, religion). In the next few chapters, we will begin to illustrate this heterogeneity by comparing and contrasting the experiences of two hypothetical clients as we more thoroughly describe the systems of inequality and subsequent impact on identity development (racism, caste system, and patriarchy).

The two hypothetical clients presented here are based on the authors' clinical experiences, personal experiences, and conversations with other Asian Indians with diverse intersectional identities. With the intent of having more diverse voices represented in this book, the authors reached out to Asian Indians with diverse intersectional identities in order to be able to describe a broader range of experiences within this population. Please note that these two case vignettes do not represent the experiences of all Asian Indians, and it is beyond the scope of this chapter (and of the authors' own experiences) to encompass the full range of experiences within this population. Thus, we encourage you to use these examples as stepping stones to consider how else identity development and mental health experiences may unfold for Asian Indians in the United States.

Anaisha

Anaisha identifies as a 40-year-old Indian American (Desi), Christian, low-caste, queer, cisgender female who currently resides in Southern California. Anaisha is currently employed as a sous chef at a two-star

Michelin restaurant. Anaisha has been married to her partner, Noor, for the past 6 years but they have been together for the past 10 years. Noor identifies as a South Asian, Muslim, bisexual, cisgender female whose family immigrated from Bangladesh. Anaisha and Noor have two adopted children (aged 3 and 5).

Anaisha was raised in a family unit that consisted of both biological parents, who are married, and two younger siblings (brother, aged 34, and sister, aged 28). She was born in Kenya and immigrated with her parents and her younger brother to New York when she was 12 years old. Anaisha's younger sister was born and raised in the United States. With regard to family history, Anaisha's father was born and raised in Nairobi, Kenya, while her mother was born and raised in the northwest regions of India (Gujarat). Anaisha's paternal grandparents and family migrated to Eastern Africa as laborers during the 1950s. In New York, Anaisha and her family lived in a low-income, predominantly Black and Brown neighborhood, isolated and feeling alienated from both South Asian and non-South Asian communities. Her low-income background, compounded by her caste identity and sexual identity, as well as immigration differences, significantly impacted Anaisha, who struggled with finding community within predominant South Asian and non-South Asian spaces. Further, being the oldest child and a first-generation college student has significantly shaped her experiences and interactions with her family and American society. Experiences of social isolation, relationship difficulties, and identity-related concerns, manifesting through psychosomatic presentations (e.g., frequent migraines, muscle tension, nausea), are concerns that she has and continues to struggle with.

Samar

Samar is a 19-year-old, second-generation Indian American, single, queer and assigned-male-at-birth (AMAB), genderfluid individual who uses he/him pronouns and is actively exploring both gender and sexuality. Samar was born and raised in a conservative, middle-class Asian Indian household in a conservative and primarily White community in the United States. He is an only child in an intact household and describes his relationship with his parents as amicable. While some of his extended family practices Hinduism, Samar and his parents are nonreligious. Samar's parents have an intercaste marriage, and while caste was not a large part of his identity throughout his childhood, there are certain aspects of his life in which it has felt more salient, such as in his interactions with the paternal side of the family, who are more religious. Samar reports having always felt out of place in his communities—there was always something about him that set him apart from others in his home and in his school. Now in his second year as an undergraduate at a large, public university, Samar is exposed to a wider diversity of identities and ways of being. He does not live at home with his parents, and conceptualizes this independence as an opportunity to explore his own identity. Samar is seeking therapy to address concerns about his identity development and changing relationships with members of his family.

2

Racism

Introduction

What would American society look like if it was designed without a **racial hierarchy**? What if everyone in American society—regardless of their race, ethnicity, and immigration histories—had equitable status in society, where access, privilege, and challenges were the same for everyone? People would likely still develop cultural biases, but individual cultural appraisals would not have the systemic power to marginalize specific communities in America. Such idealistic thinking can help elucidate how race in American society is a superordinate variable that dictates individual and community realities through the racial hierarchy, and whose impact is further compounded by other intersecting identities (e.g., gender, caste, socioeconomic class, sexual orientation, and religion).

Racial minorities in the United States are unwittingly measured against the "White norm," which determines how one's name, communication preferences, family structures, ancestral practices, and traditions are perceived, judged, and treated. Therefore, cultural practices and rituals are perceived as "abnormal," "strange," or "exotic" if they significantly deviate from Eurocentric culture. American history is therefore witness to cultural genocide in every century through the forced assimilation of racial and ethnic minorities who often sacrifice their cultural identities in order to survive and be accepted by American society. These messages about what is and is not acceptable can be internalized by communities of color, who may then reject their own cultures and sociocultural identities or separate themselves from their communities as a way to claim "difference" from the stereotyped markers.[1]

Mental health professionals can often inadvertently reinforce this White supremacist system when they use Eurocentric norms to assess normality, boundaries, and dysfunction in their racial and ethnic minority clients and their families. When we use the "White cultural norm" to assess diverse clients (which can occur colloquially or officially through the use of diagnostic tools and assessments), we perpetuate the marginalization of our clients by stifling their ancestral wisdom and intergenerational traumas, cultural upbringing, and their multifaceted identities. Asian Indians are a community with a constellation of unique migration stories, ancestral cultural practices, beliefs, and traditions. As emphasized in Chapter 1, the aim of this book is to help liberate mental health professionals from Eurocentric (Western) frameworks by way of rejecting the White cultural norm in order to support racial and ethnic minorities to be their own cultural norm.

In the first chapter, we provided an overview of the cultural context that has shaped the Asian Indian population. In this chapter, we will explore, through two in-depth cases, the multifaceted nature of Asian Indian experiences that are a result of the intersection between different sociocultural identities, immigration histories, and racial socialization. Refer to the case description section prior to this chapter for a quick reference on the background information for each character.

Anaisha

Between Three Cultural Worlds: Struggles With Identity Consolidation

Western society often revels in putting individuals into boxes, which became part of how European colonizers maintained systemic power and control over each community they came into contact with over the centuries. This tendency translates into asking individuals how they identify themselves, and (for individuals of Asian descent in particular) where they come from. This can be a complex answer as even individuals of Asian descent who are born and raised in the United States are perceived as perpetual outsiders or foreigners. In this way, American land is often associated with Whiteness despite the fact that all American soil is sacred Indigenous land that has been stolen and occupied over time.

It can be really difficult to feel a sense of belonging when one is considered a perpetual foreigner. This resonates tremendously with Anaisha's experiences, because she has constantly found herself caught in a web of three distinct cultural worlds: having been born in Kenya and spending her early to middle childhood years there, then immigrating to New York as a teenager, in addition to having Indian ancestry, the constellation of Anaisha's identity has always been evolving. Depending on the context, she has tried to be "more American," "more Indian," and has also engaged in situational adaptation to accommodate and blend in with the people she is around. In addition to feeling a lack of belonging, it can also be difficult for individuals such as Anaisha to develop a strong sense of their identity when they experience various pressures to fit into a mold, whether by American society or their families.

A common misconception is that immigrants outside of their country of origin tend to be more assimilated into the new country of residence, and that they are in this sense less attached to their heritage cultures. While this may be true for some immigrants, there are many immigrants who are more attached to their cultural roots even compared to Asian Indians residing in India or their ancestral native countries. One must remember that countries like India—which have been colonized—have experienced drastic cultural shifts as a consequence of colonization; specifically, Eurocentric ideals became valued whereas traditional Indian ideals became devalued. As a result, many Asian Indians living in India may place high esteem and aspirations toward adopting Westernized cultural norms and traditions because being "more Western" may be viewed as a status symbol. In contrast, Asian Indian immigrants sometimes have stronger ties to their heritage cultural traditions as a way to feel connected to their ancestral lands. The strong cultural ties with their native cultures can be a way to cope with the isolation and alienation that Asian Indians often experience being away from their native countries. This is also true for **twice-removed immigrants**, such as Anaisha's parents, who immigrated to Kenya and then later to the United States. Throughout her childhood, her parents expected her to be closely connected with their Asian Indian cultural roots, often demonstrating their fear of "losing" her to "Western ways."

On the other hand, American society in both explicit and implicit forms appeared to drive Anaisha toward shedding her ancestral culture through various mediums. For example, Anaisha experienced constant struggles to teach people how to correctly pronounce her name or was forced to make corrections on the stereotypical judgments about her cultural practices and traditions. Thus, whether she reacted by introducing herself as "Annie" to relieve her own irritation at others who mispronounced her name, or dismissed family traditions and cultural practices as "just an Indian thing" to Western audiences, she thought that adapting to the situational context might be a means through which she could experience a sense of belonging. This cultural adaptation process was exhausting—resulting in a sense of identity confusion and **identity diffusion** as a consequence of the constant identity switches she felt compelled to make in various contexts (e.g., family members, peers, schools, and work settings). While identity continues to develop throughout one's lifetime, there are important developmental tasks in each phase of life (e.g., infancy, adolescence, young adult) that contribute to the consolidation of one's identity, and which in turn allow for a strong sense of one's own identity and relationships with others.[2] Identity diffusion is a normal process of identity development in adolescence that can last until an individual's identity is consolidated; however, for individuals like Anaisha, identity is harder to establish due to the continuous feeling of being pulled in opposite directions. Individuals who experience identity diffusion may struggle with developing a strong sense of self or self-esteem, develop realistic self-appraisals in relation with others, and may have a higher likelihood of developing mental health concerns (Erikson, 1968; Foelsch, 2008; Goth et al., 2012).

When she first immigrated as a teenager, Anaisha struggled with fitting in with both South Asian peers and in non-South Asian spaces. Being an immigrant from an East African country distanced her from the experiences of South Asians who immigrated from South Asia, and in the same ways separated her from American-born **Desis**. This separation was also compounded by her caste background, which situated her and her family outside of the confines of mainstream South Asian American spaces. This all adds to Anaisha's feelings of alienation from both South Asian and non-South Asian communities—an aspect that has remained true for the majority of her life. Individuals such as Anaisha may present to clinical settings with a lack of a sense of who they are as a result of a lifelong journey of negotiating their identities and alienation, as well as compounding stressors as a result of the varying demands made of her by the situational contexts.

Cultural Adaptation and Generational Level

Existent scholarship is abundant with acculturation theories that attempt to explain immigrants' cultural adaptation processes. Essentially, acculturation is defined as a multidimensional process that occurs when individuals from one culture have direct and continuous encounters with another dominant culture—or, more specifically in Anaisha's case, immigrate to a country with a different dominant culture (Berry, 1997, 2003, 2005). While Berry's bidimensional (i.e., heritage culture and new dominant culture) model helps to explain some of the strategies that individuals utilize to adjust to the new dominant culture, it often fails to account for the nuances involved in this process. The model describes four different acculturation strategies: (a) marginalization, (b) separation, (c) assimilation, and (d) integration (Berry, 1997). See Table 2.1 for an illustration of how Berry's acculturation strategies may be used by someone like Anaisha.

TABLE 2.1 Using Berry's Acculturation Model to Illustrate Examples of These Strategies

Marginalization	Assimilation
Some examples include rejecting both Indian and American culture, which might result in adopting a different culture or feeling disconnected from both American and Indian society.	Some examples include mocking Indians (e.g., food), independent decision-making, rejecting cultural practices (e.g., preferring Western medication versus olive oil/honey/fennel for common colds, not wanting to wear traditional clothing), only celebrating American festivals (e.g., Thanksgiving), anglicizing one's name, and speaking only English.
Separation	**Integration**
Some examples include preferring only Indian peers, native language preferences, celebrating only Asian Indian festivals or traditions (e.g., Eid, Ali-Aye-Ligang, Diwali, Baisakhi, Christmas, Onam), and Indian food preferences.	Some examples include celebrating Indian festivals and American festivals, speaking English and native languages, wanting some family involvement as well as some independence in decision-making, choosing which elders to touch feet as a symbol of respect, using both religious scriptures and Western therapies for healing.

Clearly, a major limitation of Berry's acculturation model is that it operates from the assumption that individuals use only one acculturation strategy; however, as we have witnessed with our discussion on Anaisha's experiences, she has utilized multiple acculturation strategies at once, albeit in varying contexts. In this way, Berry's model does not fit for someone like Anaisha whose experiences with cultural adaptation are too nuanced to be simplified into one of four acculturation strategies.

Another way of conceptualizing the cultural adaptation process is via **enculturation**: unlike acculturation, which operates from the perspective of the U.S. dominant, Eurocentric culture, enculturation refers to the socialization process of one's own indigenous and ancestral practices, values, and ideas (Herskovitz, 1948). In essence, acculturation refers to how socialized an immigrant is to the U.S. dominant culture, while enculturation refers to the degree to which they have retained their own ancestral cultural knowledge and practices (Kim & Abreu, 2001). There are several benefits to conceptualizing Asian Indian clients' experiences via an enculturation lens: (a) it places an equal emphasis on their ancestral culture and practices, and (b) it considers that individuals are continuously learning, selectively retaining, and changing how they integrate their heritage cultures, mainstream culture, and influences from other cultures as result of the constant intermingling of diverse cultures within mainstream America (e.g., Desi rap, Indian American pride). It is important to keep in mind that the cultural adaptation process is often also contingent on several factors such as the (a) demographics of the state or city of residence, (b) religious identity, (c) dominant sociocultural and political climate of city or town, and (d) the degree the family practices and passes on ancestral teachings, cultural practices, and traditions to their children.

Oftentimes, mental health professionals view immigrants' experiences through the lens of challenges associated with adjusting to the host culture. In that sense, we attempt to aid immigrant clients in becoming more familiar and integrated into the host culture, often at the cost of losing connection with their ancestral practices. Upon interrogation, we can see how this practice fundamentally operates from the perspective that immigrants' wellness and well-being is dependent on the White frame of mind (and definition of wellness and well-being), rather than connection through their own indigenous culture. If, rather than an assimilation lens, we operated from an enculturation lens— involving promoting our clients' connection with their cultural heritages—we may be able to increase their cultural connection, healing, and pride with their ancestral roots. Further, it could be beneficial for mental health professionals to explore with their clients what protective function their previous adaptation strategies served for negotiating and renegotiating their identities in different spaces. Many times, individuals continue to engage in behaviors that might have previously served a positive function but that now may be harming their well-being. For example, while Anaisha previously anglicized her name (i.e., introduced herself as "Annie") to others, she may not need to do so within her current social circle, who belong to diverse cultural backgrounds. Instead, if Anaisha were to correctly pronounce her name, she might experience validation from others who have had similar experiences rather than being viewed by them as "fitting" into White norms.

Mental health professionals should also consider the **generational status** of their Asian Indian clients, as many experiences can be compounded as a result of generational status. Current research often fails to account for the varying degrees and types of stressors that individuals across different generation statuses experience. Individuals like Anaisha, who identify as 1.5 generation, experience complexities that are distinct from those of first-generation or second- and third-generation individuals. Individuals who identify as 1.5 generation are immigrants who were born in one country but grew up predominantly in a second home country—in other words, they immigrated to a second country at a young age. Many 1.5 generation immigrants frequently adopt the function of being a "bridge" between the two cultures. For example, as someone who immigrated at the age of 12, Anaisha has often found herself in the mediating role of Indian and American culture for herself and her family.

As the oldest child, Anaisha frequently had to assist her parents with navigating technology and completing paperwork (e.g., filing taxes, applying for jobs, accounting), tasks involving direct interaction with American society (e.g., navigating bills, payments, ordering food at a restaurant, speaking to a customer services representative) as well as translating American dominant cultural norms, while simultaneously learning about these norms herself. In addition, Anaisha also served as the bridge between her parents and younger siblings, who were more assimilated than Anaisha—her younger sister was born in the United States, while her brother was 6 years old (6 years younger than Anaisha) at the time of immigration. The differences between Anaisha and her siblings based on generational status manifested in growing bicultural identity conflicts between them, engendered by her younger siblings' greater degree of adoption of U.S. dominant cultural norms (e.g., preferring to speak in English rather than Hindi, desire to have increased independence, adopting westernized norms around dating and sex). Anaisha felt responsible to bridge the gap between her parents and siblings, an invisible load that she carried throughout her adolescent and adult years—a burden that those outside of the culture and Asian Indian community could not comprehend. Figure 2.1 is a visual representation of what it might look like for Anaisha to function as the "bridge" in her family and American society.

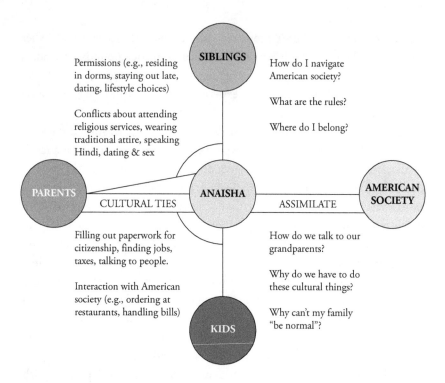

Permissions (e.g., residing in dorms, staying out late, dating, lifestyle choices)

SIBLINGS

How do I navigate American society?

What are the rules?

Conflicts about attending religious services, wearing traditional attire, speaking Hindi, dating & sex

Where do I belong?

PARENTS **ANAISHA** **AMERICAN SOCIETY**

CULTURAL TIES ASSIMILATE

Filling out paperwork for citizenship, finding jobs, taxes, talking to people.

How do we talk to our grandparents?

Why do we have to do these cultural things?

Interaction with American society (e.g., ordering at restaurants, handling bills)

Why can't my family "be normal"?

KIDS

FIGURE 2.1   Functioning as a Bridge Between Asian Indian Families and American Society

Note: Notice the complexities in the "bridging process" whereby Anaisha is navigating multiple relationships at once.

While a Western perspective on Anaisha's presenting concerns may label her relational style within her family as "interdependent" and therefore maladaptive, a mental health professional cognizant of the added complexities that a 1.5 generation Asian Indian client carries would be able to appropriately contextualize Anaisha's family dynamics and relationships without pathologizing her role in her family. Concurrently, aiding someone like Anaisha to perceive herself as an equal member of her family needing care and attention is an equally important clinical goal. It is quite common for mental health professionals to utilize "Western-informed boundaries" even when working with clients from other cultures, which serves to pathologize their heritage cultures rather than promote wellness through their culture of origin for their clients. Specifically, healthy boundaries and relational styles from a Western (individualist) perspective are different from a collectivistic culture, and clinicians may inadvertently pathologize clients who are practicing healthy boundaries and relational styles within their respective cultures. However, it can also be difficult for clinicians to accurately gauge the spectrum of healthy and unhealthy boundaries even from a culturally informed standpoint.

Racial Ambiguity: Interstitial Hyphenated Spaces

What Is Your Race?

American society has a tendency of "othering" every racial and cultural positionality outside of its confines of Whiteness. For example, surveys assessing racial demographics in the United States use race categories designated by White people (those in power) and have historically been used to frame communities as "White" versus "non-White." This type of othering through categorization is made possible through legal and systemic racial categorization. Checkboxes with predetermined identity labels often fail to account for the multilayered complexities, unique to every individual, which ultimately shape their identities.

Even as mental health professionals, we often make assumptions about our clients' identities because we think we have the requisite cultural competencies to work effectively with multicultural populations. The overestimation of one's own cultural awareness and competency can be a detriment and hindrance when working with diverse client populations. It is often helpful for clinicians, in their introductory or intake meetings with clients, to disclose their own cultural identities (e.g., race, ethnicity, gender, and other identities that are salient for the clinician) as a way to model vulnerability, equalize power dynamics with clients, and practice transparency within the therapeutic dynamic. Such cultural introductions can invite clients to "see" mental health professionals in a more authentic manner, and can allow open conversations about biases or privileges that may or may in the future influence the therapeutic working alliance.

The racial hierarchy is constructed around the White and Black racial paradigm, which leaves other racial groups in the middle with an ambiguous status. Recall our discussion in Chapter 1 of how individuals who are not White or Black (e.g., in the context of this book, Asian Indians) are often caught in the middle of the racial hierarchy where they are not clearly privileged and also not clearly marginalized; rather, they experience an ambiguous mix of both. Even within the broader Asian American diaspora, there is much debate over the inclusion of "Brown" Asians—a colloquial term describing South Asian individuals—under the label. As reflected in Anaisha's case, when she first immigrated to the United States, she felt disoriented and experienced first-hand how American society's tendency to racially and/or ethnically "box" identities affected how she navigated in and out of American society.

Anaisha has often been perceived in different ways based on the other person's preconceived notions about her physical appearance, name, skin tone, or country of origin. At times, she has been perceived as Mexican, South Asian, Muslim (often identified as a race), or biracial—all of which are inaccurate. In this sense, she has been at the mercy of others' cultural appraisals of her, rather than being able to effectively define her own existence. When one's identity is subject to constant differential perception, it can be confusing to navigate, particularly given how the racial hierarchy and intersecting constructs dictate barriers, expectations, and stereotypes. Anaisha would often try to invisibilize herself as a coping strategy to avoid distress caused by misperceptions: she would become more reserved in many spaces, focusing on others rather than her own lived experiences.

The racial hierarchical system was designed as a way to widen the wedge between Black, Indigenous, and other communities of Color in order to maintain White supremacist institutional structures. In Chapter 1, we discussed how Asian Americans—including Asian Indians—can internalize the model minority myth, the characterization of Asian Americans defined by the group's collective academic achievements and perceived upward socioeconomic mobility compared to other racial minorities.[3] In Anaisha's personal experiences, she never appeared to measure up to these "model minority" academic standards, in turn internalizing shame and guilt for being unable to "fulfill" these (societal) expectations of her. This created further separation between her and Asian American peers, including South Asians, whom she perceived as emulating the model minority standard. In a way, this reflected Anaisha's rejection of (or perceived rejection by) these Asian American identity labels.

Anaisha's identity confusion further increased when she and her family moved into a low-income, predominantly African American and Latinx neighborhood. She and her family were often viewed through the lens of being privileged because of their Asian American identity. As such, Anaisha and her family found it challenging to make connections within this community of historically marginalized and disenfranchised people whose hardships are often dismissed within the broader American society, a consequence of the Asian American model minority myth. In the same vein, her parents often forbade her to foster social connections with Black and Latinx peers in the neighborhood due to anti-Black racism that they both harbored within themselves and saw promoted in daily news programs and media outlets. Anaisha remembers often hearing her parents make statements such as "they're [Black people are] dangerous"; "it's not safe for you to visit their homes"; "focus on your studies, otherwise you will become like them."

Because she lived in a largely Black and Latinx neighborhood and had regular exposure to Black culture, Anaisha grew up regularly consuming Black artistry while simultaneously internalizing anti-Black messages from her family. This led to a confounded representation of Blackness in Anaisha's life, where she simultaneously identified with and against Black culture. For example, while her favorite musicians were Black, Anaisha had no Black friends in high school or college. While she would often use African American vernacular language, she did so with a distancing from Black people themselves. This sense of dehumanizing Black people while aggrandizing Black artists and culture is a phenomenon that is common across Asian Indian American youth, who, struggling with bridging their two cultural identities, often find medium within Black culture. While the attachment to Black culture provided a sense of connection for Anaisha to her surrounding community, it also created a paradox based on her socialization from her parents. This paradox is reflective of the larger systemic problem: that the competitive ladder that Asian Americans—including Asian Indians—strive to climb perpetuates unconscious "Oppression Olympics" (comparing who is most marginalized based on sociocultural identities) and downplaying of Black struggle.

While the model minority schema can sometimes create pride in Asian American communities due to the illusion of success or acceptance compared to other racial minorities, it can also create barriers. The previous example of how model minority stereotypes are not reflective of Anaisha's experiences was incomplete in the sense that it was missing the intersectional context of class and educational privilege, which equips upper- and middle-class Asian Indians with better resources to achieve academically. Anaisha, who came from a low-income background, was not able to afford standardized test prep courses, or extracurricular mathematics or science lessons; neither did her parents have the professional connections or financial means afforded by American-born Asian Indians or more established immigrant parents, who are able to aid their children to access better educational opportunities. Because the racial hierarchy in the United States overshadows the effects of intersectionality of other identities, Anaisha was unfairly comparing herself to peers who benefited from these educational and class privileges.

Even as an adult, Anaisha continues to experience challenges associated with others' misperception of her identities that result in the internalization of oppressive beliefs. The embedment of the racial hierarchy in American society makes it challenging for individuals like Anaisha to avoid racial microaggressions, misperceptions about their identities, or experiencing the forces of assimilation. Mental health professionals who are attuned to recognizing internalized racism and discrimination can help individuals like Anaisha realize their internalized false messages—specifically, clinicians working from a culturally informed perspective can help clients to more accurately distinguish unhealthy patterns of self-perception, and can thus be more effective in their overall healing process.

Meaning Making in the Therapy Process

There is no question that it is often challenging to assess and discern whether a behavior is perceived as "healthy," "different but not unhealthy," or "pathological." A major drawback of the mental health field is the tendency to use the same framework to assess all clients. Perceiving all clients through the same lens often decreases cultural capital,[4] and may pathologize aspects of a client's interpersonal or cultural dynamics in an unnecessary and potentially harmful way. The emerging field of multicultural counseling calls for a "decentralized" approach when working with diverse clients, whereby mental health professionals are guided by what their clients are sharing with them and their assessment of intersecting identities and culture.

Mental health professionals who practice from a decolonized lens are aware that their goal of helping clients work through mental health struggles is informed by anti-oppression practices. An anti-oppression lens means that a clinician is not only promoting their client's ancestral culture but also helping to dismantle ideologies that are harmful to them and society. Mental health professionals should balance learning about different cultures with having the cultural humility to inquire more deeply about their individual clients' identities and cultural realities. We will delve deeper into the clinical implications of working with Asian Indian clients, as well as describe further what a decolonized framework could look like, in Chapter 5.

Below are some questions related to immigration, discrimination, and internalized racism that clinicians may consider asking when working with clients like Anaisha. These questions are meant to be used as a reference and are not exhaustive of ways to develop a deeper understanding of the cultural context of Asian Indian clients. It is important to remain cognizant of the variety of family and cultural backgrounds—and degree of cultural awareness about their identities and family histories—that Asian Indian clients may have; as such, mental health professionals should phrase these questions accordingly.

Clinical Questions

1. **Who are your ancestors? [Where did your family (e.g., parents, grandparents, great-grandparents) immigrate from?]** While it may not be common practice to inquire at length about the ancestral histories of our clients, this history provides rich cultural context and intergenerational patterns within our client's cultural milieu.

2. **What is your generation status and your role in your family?** As we have witnessed in Anaisha's case, her identity as a 1.5 generation immigrant is important in her family, as she adopts the function of a "bridge" between her parents and American society as well as between her siblings and her parents. Thus, it is essential to ask clients about their immigration histories, generation statuses, and roles in their families.

3. **When you think about some of your salient cultural identities, what are some strengths and challenges associated with them?** It is common for communities of color to be perceived with a "deficit lens" that focuses on how their marginalized identities have contributed to their pain and suffering. While this type of lens is important to know and consider in understanding the experiences of various communities of color, it becomes problematic when clients' lived experiences are contextualized only through this deficit model. Thus, it is important to inquire about how their various intersecting identities also provide strength and community for them.

4. **Do you feel you are unfairly discriminated against because of your race or other identities? What helps you cope with experiences of discrimination?** Some people are aware of the discrimination they experience, while others may be used to dismissing their experiences. For example, Anaisha has internalized the discrimination she experiences by thinking of herself as "not good enough"

(Continued)

(e.g., blaming herself, viewing discrimination as occurring due to a personal flaw). Mental health professionals can empower clients by helping them identify when what their client is experiencing is discrimination, differentiating from personal flaws *and* helping clients increase their own awareness about their experiences.

5. **Do you think you are strongly attached with your culture, whether it is celebrating festivals, Indian food preferences, or speaking Indian languages?** Exploring our client's level of enculturation can provide a strong baseline of how clients may relate to their families and to the broader (in this case, Asian Indian) communities. This framework can help provide a cultural and intergenerational context for clients' presenting concerns.

Samar

As a U.S.-born Asian Indian person, Samar has spent his 19 years of life balancing being both Indian and American. His understanding of immigration is that it is something people do when they are striving to better their lives; his closest examples of this are his parents. Samar has never had explicit conversations with his parents about their immigration experiences; instead, he has gained knowledge of his parents' determination to thrive through trickle-down experiences, such as **racial socialization**, and has inherited a feeling of responsibility to uphold his parents' goals through his own success. Samar speaks English without a discernible accent; however, his parents—having moved to the United States as adults and primarily speaking Tamil and Kannada (native Indian languages)—have relatively thick accents when speaking English and are thus exposed to more frequent and explicit discrimination than Samar. Throughout his childhood, they sheltered Samar from the impact of the racism they experienced, often never sharing with him any specifics of what happened. Because children are astute, Samar was aware that something was different about his family compared with his peers' families, but without details.

When the impacts of experiences such as immigration are indirect or filtered in this way, it can be difficult for clinicians to integrate them into conceptualizations of their clients and their presenting concerns. For example, how is Samar's identity confusion tied to immigration? Does immigration count as immigration if it happened to your client's parents? Many Western psychological frameworks in the counseling and mental health fields tend to focus on individual experiences; that is, despite endorsement of the value of childhood experiences, the scope tends to be limited to the experiences of the individual client. However, not all clients are able to easily and clearly articulate their experiences with concepts that may feel indirect, veiled, or obscure to them. Even if Samar's presenting concerns are greatly influenced by a domino effect of reactions related to his parents' status as immigrants, he may not be consciously aware of it to be able to verbalize this to a clinician. Without holistic knowledge of the constructs of immigration, discrimination, and internalized racism, it could be easy to miss the nuances and underlying reasons behind Samar's accounts of feeling pressured to excel in academics, or it could be easy to overlook the depth of his difficulties with making friends in college. It would be unethical to be ignorant of the cross-generational impacts of stress and trauma associated with immigration, some of which include perpetuated discrimination and internalized racism. Thus, it is the clinician's responsibility to wonder about these things and to bring them into the conscious awareness of the client in their work.

Indirect Immigration: Looking Outside of the Individual

The way Samar was socialized to think about race and to interact with people of other races was profoundly influenced by his parents' immigration experiences and navigating the racial hierarchy in American society. Specifically, Samar's parents are used to being othered due to their immigration status; they believe their personal norms are different from "American" norms and accept that their personal values are distinct from American (rather, White) ones. Thus, they are surprised and excited when White people like Samar's friends model values and behaviors that align with Asian Indian culture—they perceive any similarities between Asian Indian and White American culture as a type of positive affirmation and acceptance. For example, throughout Samar's childhood, his parents noticed and offered praise to his White friends who described making time for dinner with their own parents, even though this was an inconsequential tradition and an expectation for Samar throughout his life.

Because they view White people as the standard for American success—a manifestation of White supremacy—it is a big deal for Samar's parents when their cultural norms are reflected in White people's behavior. However, Samar experienced praise of his White friends throughout their childhood as having an undertone of comparison with himself; on some level, his friends and peers also became his competition for his parents' approval—they were role models for success. Samar also laments the unfairness given that he would never receive praise for the things that garnered praise for his friends; he has often felt jealous of the positive dynamic between his friends and his parents, and it is hard for him to feel "good enough" for his parents' approval.[5] In reality, Samar's parents hold different standards of success for him compared to his friends due to their internalization of White supremacy: White people have already achieved success because they *are* the standard, whereas people like Samar can never achieve success—there is always a next step or standard to reach.

Success and striving for achievement are deeply rooted in the existence of the racial hierarchy and how immigrants function within the racial hierarchy system. In Chapter 1, we described the balance that Asian Indian individuals maintain between being marginalized because they are seen as inferior to White people and having privileges because they are seen as superior to other racial minorities. This is, of course, a simplistic view of the both-and balance of privilege and marginalization—in reality, it is more than just inferiority and superiority, and it is important for clinicians to spend time exploring this concept more deeply in relation to how it may manifest for our clients. In Samar's case, we know two important things: that he is a second-generation immigrant, and that his parents (who are first-generation immigrants) are important people in his life. Thus, in order to gain a truly holistic perspective on the influence of this pillar of identity development on Samar's life, we must consider Samar's parents' immigration experiences as a precursor to Samar's own experience. Samar may come to counseling settings to cope with feeling that his parents are unfairly hard on him with regard to their expectations, or that they like and appreciate everyone else more than they like him. Perhaps he feels he can never do anything right by his parents. Devoting some energy to conceptualizing Samar's parents is essential for understanding the context of his narrative, and ultimately, for helping him gain the clarity he is looking for in terms of his identity development and relationships with his family.

In terms of the racial hierarchy in the United States, the perception of Asian Indians as superior to other racial minorities is directly related to the societal perception of their success; immigrants may be socialized to believe that success is something they must achieve in order to meet societal expectations[6] and in order to avoid racial oppression. Coupled with the American cultural value of success and achievement (or what is known as the American Dream), this consequence of the racial hierarchy means that Asian Indian immigrants may experience a double emphasis on the idea that more success is equivalent to higher social standing.

People who participate in immigration begin their lives in their new country of residence already facing some barriers to success, such as language or accent differences and international educational qualifications (such as whether or not an international academic degree meets United States requirements for validity). In contrast, their children (second-generation immigrants) grow up already immersed in the new culture, and thus are seen as having an advantage and the ability to achieve greater success. Additionally, because they were born in the United States, second-generation Asian Indians' experiences are often perceived as functionally equivalent to their nonimmigrant American peers. For Samar, this means that not only does he experience an expectation of navigating American society with the same proficiency as his peers with nonimmigrant families, but he also carries an added responsibility of achieving objectively appreciable or tangible success (e.g., good grades, college and professional degrees, financially stable career) in order to maintain or improve his and his family's status within the racial hierarchy and in Asian Indian communities.

In Chapter 1, we described how non-White individuals in the United States are constantly perceived by others as foreigners; thus, their racial identity development is muddled, while intergenerational trauma responses may be clearer. The hardships that follow immigration—starting a new life in a new country, especially as a Person of Color in a country grounded in a framework of White supremacy—are traumatic, and developing a strong drive for achievement can be a reaction to this type of trauma. Intergenerational trauma means that the experiences of hardship and their respective responses are passed down from generation to generation; in this context, intergenerational trauma responses can include the heavy burden of responsibility to succeed, because the success of subsequent generations of immigrants reflects the success and legacy of the family. Clinicians may have increased difficulty conceptualizing how these responses are connected to real trauma when working with clients of later generations; however, due to the perception of non-White individuals as perpetual foreigners, the saliency of immigration trauma may not diminish with subsequent generations born in the United States. Clients like Samar, who are not directly exposed to immigration trauma, may also have trouble naming their experiences as intergenerational trauma responses. For example, Samar grew up with parents who sheltered him from the knowledge of hardship—they may have believed it was easier for Samar to simply focus on being a successful citizen without the added burden of knowing why his success is necessary. In working with Samar, it would be important for a clinician to intentionally explore how his stressors and interactions with the people who are important to him are couched in a racial hierarchical system and connected to immigration. In terms of his individual experience, it would also be important to explore how he conceptualizes being a Brown person in the United States, how he negotiates being both American and Indian, and how he copes with the role he plays in the racial hierarchy.

Both-And: Biculturality

As a second-generation immigrant in a primarily White community, Samar grew up balancing two cultures separated equally between his life at home and his life outside of home. What this balance feels like can vary for people, and it can be especially challenging to integrate cultural experiences in a way that does not feel disjointed. When the cultures in someone's life are not naturally blended—for example, in Samar's case, his house was a quite literal divide or barrier between Indian culture and White American culture—integration becomes very difficult. Some clinicians may argue that integration is not really the point, or perhaps is not a good focus for understanding biculturality, particularly if they conflate the idea of integration with assimilation. This is valid, because it can be harmful to endorse the idea that cultures *must* be blended, or that the uniqueness of multiple individual cultures must be given up in order for someone to have psychologically healthy development. However, some level of integration is also important for healthy functioning: Samar is one person with one life; even living among two distinct cultures, he has to somehow integrate them into one sense of self.

Oftentimes, the experience of biculturality is considered from frameworks of assimilation and acculturation,[7] some of which assume linear progression from one culture to another—there is a "culture of origin" and a culture to assimilate or acculturate *into*. Although these frameworks have been used to describe bicultural experiences in general, they are still inherently tied to first-hand immigration, where the introduction of multiple cultures into

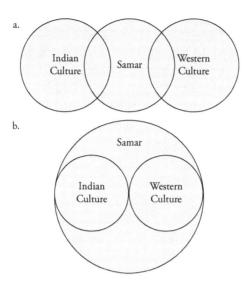

FIGURE 2.2 Illustration of Different
Conceptualizations of Biculturality

someone's life happens in a scaffolded manner—one before the other. They are
not always a good fit for people like Samar, who was born into both cultures
at once. Instead, Figure 2.2 illustrates a more applicable or helpful way for
clinicians to conceptualize second-generation immigrants. It is important that
clinicians do not independently decide which framework fits for their client but
rather that they work collaboratively with clients to explore their individual
experiences; we offer these frameworks as a starting point and alternative to
other, linear frames of thought.

Figure 2.2a reflects Samar's feelings that he is only a partial fit into both
cultures in his life. Because he is physically half a world removed from India,
he has never quite felt "Indian enough" compared to his parents, who were
born there; to him, they are representative of the Asian Indian identity label,
and he cannot measure up to them—he is too different. A clinician might
explore Samar's expectations for what it means to be Indian, including
what it is about his parents (or their characteristics) that makes him feel
like they represent "Indian-ness" better than he does and how he perceives
himself as being different from them. Based on how he was socialized in
the United States, particularly because he has limited points of reference
for what Indian people are like, Samar's perception of "Indian-ness" may be
markedly reflective of internalized stereotypes; for example, he may endorse
stereotypes that Indian parents are rigid with regard to rules and curfews, or

that they value good grades over anything else. The differences he perceives between himself and his parents (i.e., Samar resents the need for curfews and values friendships over academic performance) could have multifaceted effects on his mental health. On one hand, Samar's separation of himself from his parents is a protective mechanism against the negative stereotypes he associates with being Indian; on the other hand, this separation reinforces his feelings of not being enough.

Samar's age and the fact that he is simultaneously Western may also play a role in his negatively valenced stereotypes of Asian Indians; specifically, he is a teenager for whom independence is most easily gained through rebellion, and adopting a negative attitude toward his parents makes rebellion easier. Recalling the concept of othering as discussed in Chapter 1, Samar's implicit hesitation to identify as Indian (i.e., apprehension toward the label his parents use) could reflect internalized racism or implicit othering. Further, the culture clash between Western (Eurocentric) and Asian Indian cultures is nested in White supremacy and embodied in discrimination against Indian people; thus, Samar's negative stereotyping of his parents may also be explained as explicit othering—or perpetuating discrimination against his parents—both as an effort to be accepted by the White majority in his community and as a way to represent the Western part of himself.

This latter explanation is particularly important in the acknowledgement that Samar is just as Western as he is Indian; just as Samar grapples with feeling Indian enough, he also grapples with feeling Western (or "American") enough. Outside of his home, having been born in the United States is sometimes the only thing he feels he truly has in common with his peers. Throughout his childhood, Samar's family norms bled into his everyday life in the form of packed lunches and family nights at school, where his parents' accents all the way down to their Indian footwear were stark indicators of how he was different from everyone else, in addition to his skin color. The discriminatory attitudes he held toward his parents often paralleled the discrimination he endured from his peers; he was bullied because he was different, so he in turn blamed his parents for making him stand out to such a degree.

Because Western culture is more dominant within systems of oppression, such as the racial hierarchy, it can be easier to embrace than a more marginalized cultural identity. In Samar's case, embracing Eurocentric culture comes at the expense of discriminating against another part—the Asian Indian part—of himself. Thus, as Figure 2.2a illustrates, Samar's constant negotiation between embracing (and being accepted into) both cultures in his life, potentially to differing degrees, never completely, and sometimes at the cost of one another.

Figure 2.2b conceptualizes Indian culture and Western culture as whole and equal aspects of Samar's experience. This perspective insinuates that rather than identifying which parts of Samar fit into external definitions of these cultures, biculturality is more about acknowledging how Samar himself can define what "Indian" and "Western" mean. In other words, rather than identifying Samar as part Indian and part Western, this perspective views his experience as wholly Indian and Western. A benefit to this approach is that the cultures are not necessarily viewed at odds with one another; because the meaning of each cultural identity (i.e., what it looks like to be Asian Indian, or to be Western or American) is defined by Samar's own experience, it is expected that his manner of being Indian is informed by the fact that he is Western, and vice versa.

These two models for conceptualizing biculturality may seem to contradict; however, it is entirely possible that Samar experiences both at the same time. He may find comfort in knowing that he is a representation of an Asian Indian person and a Western American person (Figure 2.2b) while also feeling like he does not fully fit into either community (Figure 2.2a). Clinical work with Samar may involve exploring how salient each representation of identity is for him, and where his sources of comfort and discomfort are. It is important for clinicians to recognize the ways in which biculturality—or integrating multiple cultural identities into one experience—is unique for people born simultaneously into multiple cultures. Namely, framing Western culture as the dominant or destination culture, as in assimilation and acculturation theories, is harmful and inaccurate; the ability to conceptualize biculturality as a simultaneous and complex experience is pertinent to effective clinical work with this population.

Who Is an American?

Samar grew up in a family that verbalizes differences between Indian and American people. Samar's parents interchange "White" and "American": throughout his childhood, they would say "American friends" when referring to his White friends. Perhaps because they are first-generation immigrants, they experience a clear divide in cultures—there is an "us" (Indian) and a "them" (American); as their child, they may perceive Samar to be part of their own group regardless of Samar's individual identity. Parents' perceptions of their children are often reflected in how they socialize them. By referring to his White friends as American, Samar's parents gave him two messages: that he is different from Americans, and that Americans are White.

For someone born already immersed in two different cultures and identifying to some extent with both, this type of socialization can be incredibly confusing. In fact, these messages about who is and is not American perpetuate Samar's feelings of contention and inadequacy in relation with his parents: he rejects his parents, who do not see him as American and who approach his nonstereotypically Indian qualities with criticism, and he harbors fear that his parents reject him for failing to live up to their standards of belonging under the Asian Indian umbrella.

Implications of childhood socialization with identity labels are varied, and the extent to which a clinician explores this with a client will depend on how strong of a role the clinician believes childhood socialization plays in present-day experiences and therapeutic work. Do you believe that a deeper exploration of messages Samar received as a child could elucidate parallels with messages he tells himself today about where he belongs—and with which identity labels he belongs—in society? Alternatively, do you believe childhood socialization serves as a nice framework (or background) for contextualizing Samar's current presenting concerns? Much of the information presented here is about things that clinicians may consider exploring with clients, without details of specific interventions clinicians should use. This is because a thorough understanding of Samar's background with regard to immigration, discrimination, and internalized racism can be achieved and utilized for effective therapeutic work in innumerable ways; it is important for clinicians to remain cognizant of what they hold to be true about the phenomena of suffering and healing.[8]

So, How Do You Actually Do It?

It is hard to know exactly where to start when it comes to practicing social justice-oriented and conscious psychotherapy as a clinician. Since race and racism are sensitive topics, it may be difficult to bring them up organically in a session. Thus, a clinician's voyeur into incorporating **systemic** and intersectional work—clinical interventions that explicitly acknowledge the impact of systems of oppression on the individual—may begin with psychoeducation rather than with exploratory questions. A clinician may need to establish that they are actively social justice oriented in order to create a safe space for the mutual vulnerability that is required for effective clinical work. Incorporating psychoeducation will be discussed further in Chapter 5; however, we also acknowledge that good clinical work often stems from effective questions. Thus, we offer some basic questions here (in no particular order) for how a clinician working with a client like Samar might approach issues of immigration, discrimination, and internalized racism, and their connection with identity development.

Clinical Questions

1. **When you consider your identities, what comes up for you when you think about your race compared to your culture?** This question can help assess how much of Samar's cultural experience he ascribes to the way his race is categorized in the United States. It may lead to conversations about Samar's perceived acceptance or level of fit into different racial and cultural groups.

2. **Which of your identities currently feel most salient for you?** This question can help assess Samar's intersectional experience and establish a safe space for conceptualizing and exploring the different dimensions of his identity. If relevant, the clinician may provide more guiding follow-up questions related to race, ethnicity, and culture.

3. **Your parents are immigrants, and you are not. How do you think this may have impacted you while you were growing up?** This question invites Samar to consider the differences between himself and his parents. Since this is an established stressor for Samar, the clinician may use tentativeness ("may have") to impart empathy and focus ("how do *you* think") to center Samar's personal experience and help him to be in control of his narrative.

4. **What was it like to be the only Indian person in your group of friends or in your school?** This question is grounded in curiosity and again invites Samar to share his narrative with the clinician. In this way, the power to

(Continued)

tell his story and to explore the impacts of his experiences within systems of oppression lies with Samar.

5. **Throughout your childhood, what messages do you remember receiving about the racial hierarchy and racism in the United States?** This question allows Samar and the clinician to begin exploring Samar's conceptualization of the racial hierarchy. The clinician may consider the ways in which their own thoughts about the hierarchy are similar or different from Samar's, and how this may play a role in the therapeutic collaboration.

3

Indian Caste System

Introduction

For centuries, the Hindu caste system—engineered as a system of social control—has enabled violence and oppression of millions of Dalit, low-caste, and religious minorities on the Indian subcontinent. Ancient Brahmanism scriptures have determined who is deemed to be "upper-caste" and who is "lower-caste," or worse, who should be cast outside of the system altogether. The Indian caste system has created and continues to perpetuate intergenerational wounds of suffering, marginalization, and exclusion.[1] These wounds are inflicted not only on individuals oppressed by the Hindu caste system but also on those who benefit from it. *When we inflict wounds on another, whether intentional or not, we become involved in the wounding process.* The lack of awareness of caste-based wounds of upper-caste Asian Indian Americans has not permitted the healing and evolution from this system of social control. Mental health professionals with a caste-based foundation can aid both upper-caste, lower-caste, and Dalit communities in healing from intergenerational wounding as well as help communities become liberated from this system of social control (by accepting its existence).

When we think of the racial hierarchy, akin to racial caste, it is easy to notice how race permeates every aspect of American society. Whether it is in the criminal justice system, housing and employment infrastructures, or health care networks, racial caste determines differential access and barriers that impact every member of American society. Similarly, the Indian caste system is deeply embedded within Asian Indian communities. Unlike physical determinants (such as skin color) afforded to the racial caste system, the Indian caste system is too complex to easily discern even though caste categories do, to an extent, fall along color lines. In other words, colorism is a method that some people use to try to determine

69

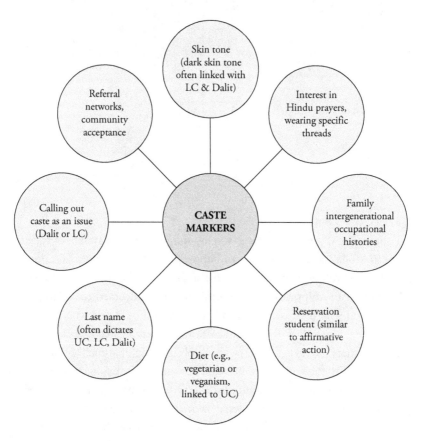

FIGURE 3.1   Common Markers Used to Identify One's Caste Identity

Note: LC = lower caste; UC = upper caste.

caste status—but, as discussed in Chapter 1, an individual's caste background can be discovered through various other methods (refer to Figure 3.1 for some examples of caste markers).[2]

The salience of a caste identity, then, is a matter of privilege and is indicative of who has enough privilege to not have to think about their caste status (similar to White privilege). Those marginalized within and outside of the caste system are forced to think about their caste identities whether they want to or not, because their caste identities dictate barriers with regards to finding community, and having benefits of informal social and referral networks, intergenerational wealth, marriage alliances, and navigating caste discrimination.

An individual's caste identity dictates access and barriers as well as several integral aspects of being able to thrive in society—but there is often a tendency to view South Asian ethnic communities as monolithic, which perpetuates the invisibility of the sociocultural complexities within these societal microcosms. Perhaps this stems from striving for stronger acceptance of ethnically diverse communities: "We are all the same, let us learn to love each other." While such notions can appear as attempts to be more inclusive, they ultimately end up maintaining these exclusionary practices. Western society's perception of Asian Indian communities as collectivistic and homogeneous disguises the differences among Asian Indian community members and often the caste and color divides within the community's infrastructure.

Asian Indians across international borders also tend to dismiss caste as a major issue within their cultural practices, often unaware themselves of how they perpetuate the caste hierarchy through marriage proposals, caste-based Ayurveda cookbooks,[3] workplace discrimination, household helpers, and color-based stereotypes. Further, many Asian Indians may object to the power of the caste hierarchy and yet still subscribe to practices that maintain caste-based boundaries. That being said, the suppression of the caste system is not always due to a lack of awareness—it is also often an aspect of conscious decision-making in order to preserve a positive and flourishing cultural image of Asian Indians in American society (and sometimes having an upper-caste status is a matter of pride within families and communities).

When we think of the struggles that non-White racial and ethnic minorities face with regard to their inclusion and acceptance in American society, it is unsurprising that Asian Indians might want to suppress darker aspects of their cultural and religious practices. It is easier for Asian Indians to feel pride when cultural elements such as yoga, Indian traditional outfits (saris, salwar kameez, kurtas), or henna are exoticized (a distorted version of acceptance) by non-Asian Indians. Thus, it is not uncommon for many Asian Indians to feel excited when non-Asian Indians seem to be in awe of their religious or cultural practices. In contrast, there are other aspects of Asian Indian culture such as the caste hierarchy that are not so easily accepted, appropriated, or admired by Western society. Due to the striving for acceptance, these cultural components may be ignored, avoided, or suppressed.

Even Asian Indians who advocate against racialized capitalism that tends to occur via "white-washing" or exoticization of cultural practices, such as yoga (and are therefore seemingly less enamored with cultural acceptance by Western society) rarely call out casteism within their own families or communities. This stems from the fear that if White Americans were to learn of the "nonexotic" or less awe-inspiring elements of their religion or culture, their perseverance and collective successes as model minority immigrants would be dismissed. Underlying the suppression of caste are the Asian Indian cultural values of saving face and secrecy, without which Asian Indians believe their status has no value.[4] Thus, secrecy and silence are often adopted around caste, whether it is upper-caste Asian Indians, who attempt to suppress the spreading of information around oppressive cultural elements such as caste, or Dalit and low-caste Asian Indians, who may practice silence around caste in order to protect themselves and their families from discrimination.

As illustrated, the caste system (and, thus, caste identities) are quite dynamic and complex. It is beyond the scope of this chapter to describe all of the multilayered experiences that Asian Indians may have. However, as an introduction to the various manifestations of caste, we hope this chapter will provide a foundation for readers to reflect on this pillar of Asian Indian identity development and consider how it may interact with the others discussed throughout this book. We further encourage readers to consider the multidimensionality of caste: outside of caste identity within the hierarchy (upper caste, lower caste, or Dalit), individuals may differ on the extent to which they believe caste impacts their daily lives, their knowledge levels about caste, and their direct and indirect experiences with caste discrimination.

Anaisha

How Caste Operates Outside of the Indian Subcontinent

Anaisha's family belonged to a low-caste group called "Dhobis" (cloth washers), who are essentially at the bottom of the caste hierarchy (some who identify with this subcaste will identify as Shudra or Dalit). Recall from Chapter 1, the caste system places Brahmins at the top and Shudras at the bottom of the hierarchy. Many Asian Indian communities often identify or are identified by others in the community by their subcaste categories, which are still defined via occupations but the language/name differs based on geographical regions in India that individuals are from (hence there are hundreds of subcastes). Thus, Asian Indians will typically not identify with the general caste categorical names unless they belong to the Brahmin caste.

As previously described, Anaisha was born in Kenya and lived there until she was 12 years old prior to immigrating to the United States. Many Asian Indians who immigrated to Kenya were known to settle in the city of Nairobi; thus, the city has a thriving population of Asian Indians who have been residing there for decades. Anaisha and her family experienced first-hand how the Hindu caste system manifests outside of the Indian subcontinent. To community outsiders, the small Asian Indian community in Kenya appears as a supportive and closely bonded community; however, these outsider perceptions belie the separation and caste lines occurring within the community.

The majority of Asian Indians who are typically able to immigrate to other countries, including African countries, have mostly been upper-caste Asian Indians—a consequence of intergenerational privileges through education, occupation, and wealth accumulation. Thus, families such as Anaisha's who belong to lower castes or are Dalit tend to be very few in number. Anaisha recollects attending major festivals with her family at the Indian community hall and thought everyone "was the same." As she grew older, she began to realize that her close friends and their families were often invited to parties that she and her family were not invited to. Anaisha later realized that these were "caste exclusive" parties—only for people who belonged to a certain (higher) caste and socioeconomic class. Anaisha describes the first time she learned about caste-exclusive parties as feeling like a bucket of ice-cold water was poured onto her; while she considered some of the attendees to be her friends, her parents' hesitation and over protectiveness began to make sense.

During Anaisha's adolescent years, her mother often told her stories of the intergenerational cloth-washing occupations that have been in their family and also of how caste discrimination manifested in their experiences. For instance, her grandmother was not allowed to use the bathroom when she worked as a household helper for upper-caste families. Further, Anaisha's grandmother was not permitted to enter the temples in her employers' homes due to the perception that her presence would make the temple "impure." It is not uncommon for upper-caste families to eat indoors while low-caste and Dalit individuals eat outside, even when they are working at the same place. Her grandmother's experiences date back 50 years from present day—showcasing that casteism is a far cry from being an ancient practice.

Anaisha's rising awareness of casteism led her to convert to Christianity in her late adolescent years as a way of rejecting the practices of Hinduism that have oppressed her family and others for centuries. However, Anaisha has consciously avoided Indian-predominant churches, as she has found that casteism often manifests within these churches as well.

One might argue that perhaps the close-knit Asian Indian community in Kenya is an outlier compared to other Asian Indian communities outside of the Indian subcontinent and that casteism is not practiced by the majority of Asian Indians outside of the Indian subcontinent. However, casteism functions in similar ways in the United States as well. Unlike the explicit nature of casteism in India, casteism in the United States operates similarly to present day racism—in an implicit and subtle manner. After immigrating, Anaisha's parents were often greeted with "superficial niceties" by higher-caste Asian Indians in community gatherings; they did not receive the same preferential treatment, openness, and sharing of resources and opportunities that those within the same caste would receive. Thus, rather than simply not being invited (or being explicitly excluded) from such gatherings, they experienced discrimination that was more passive-aggressive in nature.

Caste-based discrimination among Asian Indian workforces is also a common occurrence, but it is masked to cultural outsiders who are unaware of caste markers that operate similarly to racial markers (Figure 3.1).[5] Asian Indians in engineering or technical fields, where Asian Indians predominate, commonly face caste-based discrimination and experience caste-based slurs. However, due to the lack of awareness that non-Asian Indians or non-South Asians have of casteist practices (common among 1.5, second-, and third-generation South Asians), caste-based discrimination tends to be invisible compared to other types of discrimination (such as racism and sexism).

The above examples reference Asian Indians who are cognizant of their casteism, but there are many upper-caste Asian Indians who lack conscious awareness of the casteism that they practice in their daily lives. These are Asian Indians who may have internalized caste-based messages without being consciously aware of how it is operating in their lives. For example, an Asian Indian person sharing a caste-based joke (e.g., making fun of low-caste or Dalit individuals) may dismiss it as "humor," or as not a true reflection of their thoughts. This is similar to how some people with racial privilege consider racist jokes to be acceptable because they are not intended to harm anyone.

Another example of how unconscious casteism can manifest is through matrimonial alliances, where family members explicitly state their caste preferences for a potential partner for their children. In Anaisha's case, she has often noticed how people would retract interest in her younger sister after seeing her biodata or after finding out about their family history with regard to caste. Some biodatas will even explicitly include a preference for "Brahmin" or name a specific subcaste preference.

Further, if an Asian Indian person engages in any kind of indecent behavior that is viewed as disgracing the Asian Indian community (including, but not limited to, being convicted for a criminal or other offense), the first question asked by someone discussing this within their community might be "where are they from [what is their caste]?" However, people generally deny having a casteist mindset or that their opinions are influenced by caste. These examples illustrate that contrary to the majority of upper-caste Asian Indians in the United States denying caste as a major marker in their experiences, casteism is deeply embedded into the culture, both in the Indian subcontinent and in international Indian diasporas.

Internalization of Caste-Based Schemas

The practice of casteism can have significant negative effects on Asian Indians' psychological well-being, self-esteem, and motivation level to overcome barriers, which are unseen to the majority of other Americans. Asian Indians may internalize casteist messages and interpret them to describe personal flaws rather than as a manifestation of the oppression they experience in the caste system. Further, Asian Indians who fall outside of caste boundaries or who belong to low-caste backgrounds may experience isolation because their caste status does not permit them to be included in the "elite" caste and class system, in turn preventing them from finding community within larger Asian Indian communities in their city or state.

As mentioned in Chapter 1, caste is not limited to Hinduism; these systemic patterns also manifest across other religions due to the widespread influence of the caste system in South Asia. This is why it is important for mental health professionals to have a foundational framework of the Hindu caste system—*and* to be aware of how the system prevails when disconnected from the actual religion—because its invisibility conceals both the psychological and societal harms against Asian Indians.

Due to the insidious nature of the caste system, it is often not something that is easily reflected in Western counseling intake paperwork; rather, it may come out of an in-depth assessment completed by a mental health professional. In other words, assessing caste and the ways in which it influences a client may need to be a more intentional endeavor on the part of a clinician rather than relying on typical questions about culture that may be included in standard Western intake paperwork. Below are some example questions that mental health professionals can use to learn more about their Asian Indian clients.

Clinical Questions

1. **How do you and your family relate to (or not relate to) Asian Indian community members?** Inquiring about an Asian Indian person's positionality and how they relate to other Asian Indian community members can reveal information about any within-group differences between your client and the Asian Indian community in their area.

2. **How have you experienced caste discrimination in Indian community settings, potential partners, or work or academic settings by other Asian Indians?** Since caste discrimination is not legally or socially recognized in the United States, it is often invisible to those who do not experience it. Thus, a mental health professional might be the first person to inquire about caste discrimination and in turn be able to validate a client's experiences in this way.

3. **What stories do your parents/grandparents tell you about Asian Indian communities and their positionality and status?** When we meet with clients, we cannot isolate their experiences from everything that has shaped them. Individuals are often shaped by generations of family relationships and patterns, migration histories, trauma, and culture; inquiring about this in therapy settings can provide enriched information about the potential impacts on our clients. Asking Asian Indian clients about their family histories and ancestral stories will thus reveal a lot about them as individuals. Even when Asian Indian clients are unaware of the details of their family histories, this is a way to gather data about their privilege or marginalized statuses within their communities.

4. **What are your family's migration stories?** This question can provide information about the client's family. Migration stories often reveal the complexities (e.g., privileges, resources, barriers) with how individuals

participate in immigration or the circumstances that allowed them to do so. It enables the client to also decide how much they want to share with you.

Samar

As described in the previous section, Asian Indians in the United States may have a different understanding of caste based on their immigration histories, family background, caste status, and other intersecting identities, reflecting the heterogeneity of their experiences. This section illustrates how a caste identity can still be relevant and impactful for an Asian Indian person even if they have less conscious awareness of how it is functioning in their lives.

Since Samar was born and raised in a predominantly White community in the United States and does not have substantial grounding in Asian Indian history or a close connection with the culture, his knowledge of the caste system is extremely limited compared to his knowledge of racism and the racial hierarchy. While Samar's environment socialized him to the racial hierarchy due to direct and indirect experiences of racism, he lacked awareness of the caste system because he did not have Asian Indian peers or cultural environments that facilitated education or connection with Asian Indian culture. This comparison further highlights the divide between Samar's life inside and outside of his home; while his caste identity is not the most salient for him in general, it does inform his interactions within his family system, whereas his racial identity is more salient for his interactions with his peers and neighbors. Even within Samar's home, however, caste is more prevalent with regard to his parents' identities rather than his own. While he is aware of his parents' intercaste marriage, Samar perceives himself as somewhat of an outsider to the groups (castes) his parents belong to.

Because he feels one step removed from caste, it can be challenging to clearly identify the different ways in which caste is prevalent in his life. As a system of oppression, caste can function as an underlying framework even when it does not feel important—in Samar's case, the influence of caste background on his experience is in his conscious awareness in some contexts (e.g., within his family) but not in others (e.g., among his peers). A goal of clinical work may then be to help a client understand the reasons behind their presenting concerns, to answer the "why": *Why* am I having this problem? Or, *Why* is my life like this? It is possible that sometimes the answer may be related to caste background; an indirect effect can still be a significant influence on a person.

Perhaps a client like Samar may not have much to say about caste due to the lack of awareness of how caste might have shaped his or his family's lived experiences. If you ask, "What do you know about your family's caste background?" they may not have much of a history to give. However, even this lack of information is data that can be used in clinical work. It can be useful to take the perspective that every part of a client's experience serves a function for them; if a client does not know about a part of their history, why might that be? There may be something to explore there. Further, caste, like race, is a social construct, which means there is no single "right" way to define the system or its categories. A basic understanding of how a client might conceptualize caste itself is critical to the assessment of how it plays a role in their identity development and overall mental health.

Gaps in Knowledge

Samar knows what caste is, can name some caste groups, and can recite some facts about his parents' different caste backgrounds: namely, that his father descends from Vaishyas—merchants and landowners—while his mother descends from Shudras, generations of farm and household workers. For Samar, these facts live in a compartmentalized area in his brain—information he feels no personal connection to. He has a similar experience with religion. While his extended family practices Hinduism, Samar's parents socialized him to be nonreligious; his knowledge of Hinduism is in isolated bits, like stories from a storybook. This has perpetuated the feeling of disconnection or lack of belonging with his extended family, who find caste and religion to be much more salient. For example, his cousins regularly watch television serials about the *Mahabharata* and the *Ramayana*,[6] and Samar constantly feels like he is missing out due to not having the context necessary to fully participate in their conversations. Consequently, he often finds himself isolated and marginalized by them.

Since the caste system has roots in Hinduism, the religious divide between his immediate and extended families informs Samar's sporadic experience with caste and casteism. But what function does this lack of experience or gap in knowledge serve for Samar? In Chapter 1, we described the ways in which some people disassociated from Hinduism as a way to escape the caste system. Although it would be difficult to ascertain his family's situation and the reasons behind his parents' decision to forgo conversations about caste and religion, we can hypothesize that his parents may have chosen to avoid discussions about religion and caste in their household due to their experiences of discrimination within their families. In other words, Samar's lack of socialization about caste and religion could be due to his parents' attempts to protect him from negative experiences. Informed hypotheses like this, which are grounded in a thorough understanding of how the impacts of systems of oppression can manifest in individuals' lives, are integral to meaningful therapeutic work with clients. The ability to hypothesize in this way based on a foundational knowledge of caste could prevent clinicians from inadvertently oversimplifying and labeling a client's socialization as "maladaptive." Consider conceptualizing Samar's parents' experience with interfamilial caste discrimination as a type of trauma. Sociocultural experiences that enforce and perpetuate systems of oppression cause severe distress for affected individuals and trigger response patterns that parallel the manifestation of other known types of trauma.[7] Note that every reaction a person has to trauma serves a function for them, whether to help them heal, cope, or simply survive. From this perspective, Samar's parents' avoidance of discussing certain identities (such as religious identity) and systems (such as the caste system) can be seen as a trauma coping mechanism. A clinician aware of and competent with navigating these complexities could avoid leading Samar to label his parents as "bad parents" and instead help him to find a balance between recognizing his parents' caste-based trauma and managing the trickle-down effects on an individual level.

I'm Confused: Intercaste Discrimination and Family Dynamics

Despite his parents' desire to shield him from intercaste discrimination, Samar still witnessed both personal and secondhand discrimination within his family dynamics. Extended families subscribing to the caste system expressed serious discontent with his parents' union: Samar's paternal family accused his father of "marrying down," while his maternal family approached the marriage with distrust and skepticism (i.e., "He must have an ulterior motive for marrying below his caste; perhaps he wants to enforce power over his wife"). For Samar, this resulted in a spectrum of experiences from lack of acceptance to explicit discrimination from both sides of his extended family.

Growing up, Samar noticed differences in how his parents were treated by their respective in-laws (Samar's grandparents) compared with how his grandparents treated his aunts and uncles who were of the same caste.

Specifically, Samar shares that he does not have many positive memories of the relationship between his paternal grandparents and his mother. He is generally of the opinion that his paternal grandparents do not like his mother, though he has never been able to pinpoint a particular reason why that might be; their dislike has been subtle rather than explicitly hateful or discriminatory. For example, Samar notices that the patriarchal gender role expectations for his parents become more apparent whenever his grandparents visit from India. Their visits always seem to multiply the amount of time his mother spends in the kitchen or in her bedroom, and they are rarely in a room together unless his mother is engaged in an act of service.

Samar also perceives a certain distance between his paternal grandparents and himself that does not exist for others in his family, like his cousins. For example, Samar's grandparents offer more praise and gifts to his cousins than to Samar because of their mother's higher caste background: they often give his cousins new clothes for religious holidays, whereas Samar is gifted hand-me-downs used by other family members. Samar's grandparents also maintain relationships with the parents of their children's spouses who are of the same caste, and invitations for big family events are sent to everyone connected to the family; in contrast, the maternal side of Samar's family is never invited to these events due to their lower-caste status.

Although Samar is aware of the uncomfortable dynamics within his family, he attributes these to cultural differences, where he perceives his paternal grandparents to be "more Indian" than his immediate family. Samar believes his parents are typically more egalitarian because of the Western influence of living in the United States, and his frustration with the oppression of his mother translates to a disdain for some parts of Asian Indian culture. Although the family dynamics are likely a result of a combination of things (e.g., sexism, casteism, sociocultural environments, personality types), acknowledging the casteism can provide additional context for clinicians to help Samar explore how he is personally impacted by these relationships. For instance, what are some messages Samar might internalize about himself and his family based on these interactions? It is clinically relevant to take a developmental perspective on the impact of family dynamics on children. Children learn how to interact with society based on watching those closest to them and internalizing how their caregivers are perceived by the community. To an extent, Samar thinks of his parents as representations of himself, and how they are perceived by their community is also a reflection of him. Thus, the messages he has received from his extended family throughout his childhood, based on how his mother is treated by paternal relatives, may be that he represents a tainted part of the family bloodline. Additionally, given his maternal family's distrust and skepticism toward his father, Samar may internalize messages that he, too, is untrustworthy.

"Tainted" and "untrustworthy" are strong words to describe a client's experience, and it can feel pertinent to explore the mental health effects of such messaging; however, it is also important for a clinician working with Samar to maintain the perspective of the larger picture, which is that Samar does not view caste as a primary identity influencing his daily life. There is a balance to be found between acknowledging the serious impacts of discrimination and recognizing the indirect or covert ways they may emerge in Samar's life. Thus, it may not be clinically appropriate to explore the direct relationship between caste discrimination and identity development the way in which a clinician might with other clients. Instead, clinical work should explore a client's expectations and **schemas** and assess caste as an undercurrent; where it fits as a potential explanation for a client's experiences, it can be introduced as an intervention for building insight with a client.[8]

Residual Effects of Caste: Education and Career Choices

We have established that when people experience caste as a secondary or nonsalient identity, they may not be aware of how their caste background operates to affect their daily lives. Let's explore caste as an undercurrent of Samar's life outside of his family dynamics. As a second-generation college student, Samar's struggles with deciding on a major field of study are relatively normal. On the surface, this is a shared experience with many other college students his age: Samar finds it difficult to integrate his personal interests with a feasible career. How might knowledge of the caste system provide a useful framework for a clinician working with Samar on academic and career concerns? As we discussed in Chapter 1, occupational categories underlie the hierarchy of the caste system. Although it is not unlike the capitalistic view of occupations in the United States, where service-related jobs are stigmatized, the caveat of the caste system is that there is no mobility across categories. Caste discrimination enmeshes people's humanity with occupations, and stigma exists against people as individuals and against careers.

Given their experiences with caste discrimination, Samar's parents may socialize him to pursue careers that are more respected, such as in medicine or law. This may be because the lasting trauma from caste discrimination makes them fearful of a repeating pattern of discrimination with Samar, or it may be related to their own deeply held stigmas against certain occupations based on their caste status. Socialization can occur without explicitly naming caste; for example, Samar's parents may simply demonstrate more respect toward doctors than waiters, or maintain a certain occupational standard for their circle of friends.

From a Western perspective of psychology, a clinician may help Samar to build insight about how internalizing these messages from his parents could form schemas about acceptable occupations, creating a conflict between his personal interests and his expectations for himself. This is a very individualistic perspective in which the responsibility for identifying and changing problematic schemas falls on Samar and the clinician. In contrast, a cultural perspective acknowledging the caste system elucidates how occupational schemas follow intergenerational patterns and are deeply rooted in cultural history, and thus Samar's academic and career concerns are not individual in nature. Instead, clinicians should take a holistic approach that involves discussions about his family dynamics, roles, and expectations into their career exploration work with Samar.

How to Stay Cognizant of Nonsalient Identities in Clinical Work

Drawing a direct connection between caste and clinical presenting concerns before a client is ready risks halting the therapeutic work instead of helping the client increase their insight. This is because rather than fostering curiosity about the role of caste in their lives, the client might think that this topic is irrelevant to them and therefore not worth exploring. However, since we can see that caste as an undercurrent can still meaningfully impact a client's life, it can be useful to explore how we can bring this topic into the therapeutic space in an effective way. For Samar, an effective strategy may be to engage in a scaffolded exploration of caste by asking specific questions that Samar can connect to and by modeling curiosity as a therapist. Using stepping-stone questions that are easier to answer—rather than asking directly about the impact of caste on Samar's identity development and mental health—can help foster curiosity and insight instead of triggering denial from the client. Here are some examples of questions and statements a therapist might use in session:

Clinical Questions

1. **How did you learn that your parents have an intercaste marriage?** This question can help clinicians gather data about explicit messages Samar received about caste and what an intercaste marriage means to him. It may also open the door for deeper discussions about Samar's perception of unequal power dynamics between castes and within his family.

2. **It seems like your extended family has a lot of expectations of your parents. Do you feel like they have certain expectations of you, too?** This question can help clinicians bridge the gap between how Samar sees his parents being treated and the messages he internalizes about himself.

3. **I wonder what messages you received from witnessing intercaste dynamics in your family?** This open question acknowledges that his parents' intercaste background is significant, but invites Samar to verbalize in which ways it might be significant.

4. **I wonder if some of the disconnect you feel with your extended family is related to differences in caste, and how you come from a mixed-caste union.** This statement models curiosity about the role of caste in Samar's life. The goal of a statement like this could be to make curiosity about caste feel more accessible to Samar, so perhaps he can begin to feel curious about it as well.

5. **How do you think your family's history could be connected to what they think of as acceptable careers?** This open question invites Samar to explore any connections he sees between his intergenerational family history and, specifically, career expectations. This could be

(Continued)

> a segue to exploring caste dynamics in Samar's academic
> and career decisions.

Colorism: Parallels Between Whiteness, Race, and Caste

Anaisha

As illustrated previously, there are several parallels between the racial hierarchical system and the Hindu caste system. Aside from the structure and impacts of these systems of oppression, similarities are also reflected in the colorism that permeates and intertwines with the caste system. One could argue that the parallels are bidirectional—that the racial hierarchy is also a reflection of the Indian caste system, wherein lighter-skinned Asian Indians are at the top while Asian Indians with darker or dusky skin tones are at the bottom of the hierarchy (Nikalje & Çiftçi, 2021). Of course, this marriage of systems of oppression is not fully accurate as some upper-caste Asian Indians have dusky or darker skin tones and some low-caste and Dalit individuals have fair skin tones. However, due to the societal perception of lighter skin tones reflecting purity, cleanliness, and higher-caste status, anti-Blackness (and, in turn, internalized racism) are easily adopted by Asian Indians living in the United States.

This is a reflection of why "Whiteness" is a multimillion-dollar industry in Asian countries where lightening creams and fairness treatments are promoted as the "antidote" to dark skin. The fixation with fairness is especially prevalent on the gender spectrum, whereby Asian Indians who identify as women experience the worst of societal beauty standards if they are perceived as having dusky or dark skin tones. Comments such as "you will not find a husband to marry," "stop spending too much time outside in the sun," "scrub yourself better," or "try this bleach cream" are commonly heard. Further, traditional dowry practices are also heavily influenced by the bride's skin tone—the darker the skin tone, the bigger the dowry.[9]

In contemporary times, many Asian Indian dating sites and matchmaking services—even their U.S. counterparts—have categories asking about one's skin tone and skin tone preferences in their partner (e.g., fair, wheat-ish, dusky). Asian Indian activists have long been advocating for the removal of such skin tone preference categories from dating sites and matchmaking services and are slowly making progress. However, many Indian dating websites (and, on an individual level, biodatas) still continue to normalize asking for caste and skin tone preferences.

Individuals who have lighter skin tones may not realize the "light skin privilege" afforded to them. They may be ignorant of the colorist hierarchy or believe that colorism is not a problem that affects their lives. However, the subtle interplay of colorism can impact relational dynamics as well, both within and outside of Asian Indian communities. Take, for instance, Anaisha's relationship with her younger sister, who has a much darker skin tone than Anaisha: Anaisha has always perceived a rather confusing competitive streak between them. Her confusion about the dynamics between them could be related, in part, to Anaisha's ignorance of certain experiences her sister had throughout their childhood. Unbeknownst to Anaisha, her younger sister has always felt inferior to her, specifically due to having a much darker skin tone.

Anaisha, used to fielding compliments about her beauty, did not experience the side glances or whispers about how sorry people felt for her sister due to perceiving her as "less beautiful" (in other words, less fair-skinned) than her sister. Anaisha was oblivious to aunties' unsolicited advice to her sister about which kinds of facials or creams she should be using—in turn emphasizing that her sister needed to "fix herself'" because her dark skin tone is a problem. Anaisha was further unaware that her younger sister religiously applied bleach creams on her face every two weeks for years, in the hopes of striving to have a lighter skin tone. In turn, she also was not cognizant of the self-hatred and crying episodes that would follow when the only result her sister experienced was redness and irritation on her face.

The effects that these experiences have had on Anaisha's sister are explicit and clear; but how could Anaisha's ignorance of these experiences impact her own mental health and identity development? As described above, Anaisha's lack of awareness led to a gap in understanding regarding her sister's behavior and personality; this barrier to closeness could affect Anaisha's self-efficacy as an older sister. Further, without the context of how differential experiences with colorism could inform any conflict between them, Anaisha may experience sibling conflict as more distressing and confusing.

Samar

Having grown up as an only child, Samar does not experience the effects of colorism in relational dynamics with siblings. Instead, colorism is present in subtle ways in his group of friends and people he chooses to include in his social environment. Further, as he has been socialized as male throughout his life, he is sheltered from societal expectations and colorism in the beauty industry. While a common thread that Anaisha and Samar share is that they are both oblivious to any direct impact of colorism in their lives, the role that colorism plays on their identity development and mental health is quite different.

The manifestation of colorism for Samar parallels his (and his parents') internalization of the racial hierarchy. We have previously described that his parents disproportionately value White opinions and strive for acceptance from White Americans in an effort to assimilate into American society;[10] Samar also exhibits these attitudes with regard to the people he selects or pursues for friendship.

The vast majority of Samar's friends are White; while this may be due in part to the fact that he grew up in a predominantly White community, he also maintains this pattern now in college. It can be difficult to discern the difference here between perpetuation of the racial hierarchy (racism) and perpetuation of colorism; Samar's experience lies at the intersection of the two, and the colorism is present in his determination of who he likes, trusts, and interacts with. For example, while Samar tries to distance himself from other South Asians and Asian Indians due to feeling a lack of belonging in those groups, the underlying feeling behind his engagement in othering tends to fall along color lines. At his university, many South Asian and Asian Indian student groups are organized and led by lighter-skinned individuals; thus, Samar associates lighter-skinned Asian Indians with feeling intimidated based on how culturally connected they seem (i.e., he does not feel "Indian enough" for them). In contrast, he tends to perceive darker-skinned Asian Indians as "too connected" to their culture of origin, inflexible to adopting Western norms, and difficult to connect with (i.e., he perceives them as "not American enough" for him).

It is important to note that Samar's perpetuation of colorism through his more positive associations with lighter-skinned people is not simply an individual-level problem, but that it is couched in systemic colorism. Note how the distinction in his perception of lighter-skinned versus dark-skinned Asian Indians reflects who is in leadership roles. Thus, any clinical work aiming to elucidate the manifestation of colorism in a client's life should balance both individual and institutional responsibility.

Oftentimes (and particularly from a Western perspective), we believe that the goal of therapy should be about building awareness of one's own trauma and life experiences; but therapy should also be about building self-awareness about one's privilege, about colonial harms and cultural traumas, and bridging families and communities together. Without acknowledging the intersection of caste and colorism and clients' familial and social dynamics, we may continue to perpetuate the same dynamics and sociocultural harms that—if explored in therapy—can begin the intergenerational healing process.

Moving Therapy Beyond Mental and Emotional Health: Recognizing Social and Cultural Traumas

Following our critique of Western perspectives on therapy, and also to help contextualize Asian Indians' cultural and intergenerational experiences as discussed in this book, we present a reframe of the concept and definition of trauma. The propensity to view trauma as developing due to severe accidents, child abuse, sexual assault, or war is a narrow lens often endorsed in Western teachings and resources such as the *Diagnostic and Statistical Manual of Mental Disorders* (*DSM*). However, many harmful intergenerational, social, and cultural experiences that do not represent one specific event but rather chronic (ongoing) and implicit manifestations passed on ancestrally can also be conceptualized as trauma, which is a much-needed cultural discourse in the trauma framework.

Current literature has not yet fully acknowledged the significant effects that intergenerational trauma has on individuals. When people experience trauma, their families also experience the residues of this trauma through the reenactment of trauma reactions in relationships and construction of their lives around trauma. For example, individuals who have alcohol addiction or physical abuse history tend to have an intergenerational history of parents and grandparents who also experienced addiction or abuse. Along with specific stories of stress and trauma, coping and reactionary patterns are also transmitted across generations. Therefore, it is clinically important to address both the immediate individual and the ongoing intergenerational trauma experiences. Intergenerational trauma can further manifest in ways that seem subtle or superficially unrelated: research in fields such as epigenetics has begun to illustrate how an individual's stress can be transmitted intergenerationally through biological effects, which may relate to a spectrum of outcomes from personality to predisposition for disease. While most of this research still conceptualizes trauma from Western perspectives, it is also applicable and relevant to the understanding of cultural and social trauma.

More often than not, individuals live their entire lives (and families live generations) without processing their cultural and social traumas. For Asian

Indians, the unprocessed trauma impacts relationships, health, and the psychological well-being not only of themselves but also of their families and future partners and children. One example of a sociocultural trauma that impacts Asian Indians is reflected through caste genocide: centuries of psychological, social, and cultural trauma. Since caste genocide has spanned such a wide frame of time and the trauma has evolved across multiple generations, Asian Indian clients may not be aware of the true extent of the impact it has on their lived experiences. Mental health professionals can help foster increased awareness by intentional inquiry and family systems assessment (e.g., family genograms, identity flower exercise, ancestral history), psychoeducation, sharing resources on liberation text, and trauma-processing frameworks.

4

Patriarchy

Introduction

Of the systems of inequality discussed throughout this book, patriarchy is perhaps the most diffuse. On a basic level, patriarchy describes a system of hierarchy in which men hold power over people of other genders. A patriarchal society tends to be built upon male lineages, and men occupy positions of leadership throughout both institutional and individual-level communities (e.g., families). Because of the overlap between the types of oppression experienced by gender- and sexually minoritized people, over time patriarchy has also come to be understood as a system that affords power and privilege to cisgender over transgender, nonbinary, and gender nonconforming people, and to heterosexual over nonheterosexual people. Ideas about sex and sexuality, intimacy, family roles, and gender roles all fall under this broad umbrella.

Asian Indians in the United States navigate the impact of patriarchal oppression at the intersection of two worlds. While the fundamentals of patriarchy are consistent across Eurocentric and Indian cultures, immigration—and the trickle-down effect of immigration across generations—adds a unique layer to their experience. Immigration creates a rift in family structure and produces situations in which it becomes necessary for the maintenance of familial well-being for people to take on specific family roles and responsibilities. As described in Chapter 1, Asian Indian families have historically followed a joint family structure where multiple generations resided together and shared household responsibilities while maintaining an age- and gender-based hierarchy where leadership is assumed by elder male relatives. When immigration renders joint families difficult (in many situations) and impossible (in some), the burden of running a household falls on fewer shoulders to carry its weight. There may be a shift to a more egalitarian division of labor. In other cases, the gender-based hierarchy may be more explicit or salient in families that involve spousal visas, where one spouse is legally allowed to reside in the United States only because the other has a work visa sponsorship. There may be a role reversal to a certain extent where children become the knowledge bearers of Western customs, whether with regard to language, unspoken cultural norms, or systems.[1] Regardless of the details of how patriarchal inequalities can filter into Asian Indian families, readjusting family structure has an emotional and psychological cost.

Outside of family structure, systems of patriarchy often mirror each other across Eurocentric and Asian Indian societies. Some of this mirroring is prescribed and labeled, such as sexism (binary gender norms), transphobia, and heteronormativity—whole systems that are paralleled. Yet others are more nuanced, such as socialization around sexuality and physical intimacy. These manifest in things like abstinence-based sex education (which is often contrasted with shaming for not being successful or interested in romantic relationships), and regulation of girls' and women's bodies—particularly in schools—through both spaghetti straps and hijabs (for contrasting reasons). Navigating life in the United States can often feel like swimming in two streams at once—even if the water moves in the same direction, it is still taxing. Imagine the complexities of living and navigating two different intersecting cultural worlds but feeling like you do not belong to either one of them. Consider how this might impact how people perceive their identities and sense of belongingness by reflecting on the following case examples.

Anaisha

We as Americans reside in transnational societies that have a deep embedment of intergenerational sexual and gender trauma. This stems from extensive socialization compounded by the effects of colonization and heteropatriarchy that have shaped our understanding of what constitutes "normal" gender and sexuality. With regard to Asian Indians, British colonization marked a shift in the way gender was delineated in Asian Indian societies. When we consider sex and sexuality norms within the Asian Indian population, we can contextualize them in the following categories informed through patriarchy: (a) marriage, procreation, and rigid sexual norms, (b) patriarchal morality, and (c) compulsory heterosexuality. To mitigate the damages committed by colonization, then, we as a collective society have gone through centuries of unlearning what might have been normal to us with regards to how we identify, experience, and express our genders and sexualities.

Marriage, Procreation, and Rigid Sexual Norms

An interesting paradox often exists between striving for procreation and the likeness to asexual behavioral norms that have shaped and molded Asian Indian culture and society. In general, Asian Indian communities place a high value on maintaining close family relationships including marriage and procreation, which are celebrated and considered the most desired life goals. However, the path to success in either of those life tasks is never truly explored within families, nor is it encouraged for Asian Indians to engage in this kind of exploration outside of their families. Thus, this path can often be quite confusing to Asian Indian adolescents and young adults. This is even more so true for those residing in the United States: they grow up in families who have rigid restrictions around dating and relationships at home, but are also exposed to a Western society that is more open about dating, relationships, and sexual behaviors in adolescence through schools and peer relationships. Thus, it can be quite common for Asian Indian adolescents to experience the need to lead double lives—one with their families at home and another with their friends at school.

How can the perception of sex and sexuality in Asian Indian communities be so contradictory to the ascribed cultural goals of marriage and procreation? As we discussed in Chapter 1, India is often referenced as the "Land of Kamasutra," and yet Asian Indians' adopting rigid heteronormative beliefs around sex may be bewildering to many cultural outsiders. This contrast unfortunately becomes more apparent given the numerous incidents of sexual assaults and rape in patriarchal societies. The same communities that discourage sexual exploration also perpetuate sexual violence. How does one grapple with communities that can be perceived as sexually repressive but that also engage in sexual oppression simultaneously? The answer to this question lies in how patriarchy has perpetuated a pattern of sexual repression. For example, there is a historical pattern of control over Asian Indian widows' sexual and romantic desires by disallowing remarriage, as well as community condemnation of women who are sexually assaulted (but rarely the male perpetrators). The buildup of such deep ancestral and personal sexual trauma is likely to result in multiple dichotomous experiences such as those described throughout this book.

There can be serious negative ramifications on identity development and mental health for centering marriage and procreation. Oftentimes, the high pressure and expectations placed on Asian Indians to get married may result in Asian Indians deciding to get married earlier than they are ready, to forgo career-related dreams, or to miss out on opportunities to explore their sexual identities. Additionally, pressure and expectations to get married can often exacerbate stress and anxiety in Asian Indians who are constantly reminded that they are lacking or failing as adults when they have not yet accomplished these prescribed life tasks. Thus, Asian Indians may enter into relationships or marriages too quickly before fully realizing what their own expectations and understanding of relationships are or before being emotionally ready to enter into a long-term commitment. While historical records show that arranged marriages have lower divorce rates, there is also evidence that many Asian Indians stay in marriages even when their needs are unfilled, or they lack love, experience intimate partner violence, and lack compatibility. Consider this case example: given Anaisha's queer identity (discussed later on this chapter), her parents believed they waited too long to exert this pressure on Anaisha, which led her to "stray" and "adopt White people ways." Thus, her younger sister experienced increased pressure to get married earlier. Anaisha's sister would often get anxious when she would come home during her college breaks or during phone conversations with their parents because they inadvertently always brought up discussions of marriage. Anaisha's sister succumbed to this pressure and got married at 22 years of age, with no prior experience with dating, relationships, or sex. She found herself traumatized by her first sexual experience with her spouse who also had no sexual or dating experience. While this section focuses on Anaisha and her family's experience, it can be useful to also consider the harm that heterosexual men also experience as a result of the conflict between rigid sexual norms and marriage and procreation.

Morality and Physical Intimacy

In Western and Asian Indian conservative cultures, sex and physical intimacy are codified and intertwined with certain beliefs about morality. Specifically, morality is associated with the controlling and confinement of sexual desires and physical intimacy until marriage. Outside of cultural norms and expectations for engagement (or nonengagement) in intimacy, morality bleeds into everyday life and interactions. Anaisha remembered the deep discomfort among her and her family members while watching

Bollywood romantic scenes during her childhood. A far cry away from a scene depicting sex, a mere almost-kiss would result in her parents fast-forwarding the scene in the movie.

Morality also includes policing women's bodies. An aunt once remarked to Anaisha that she should not wear tank tops or shorts because girls who wear such clothes are sexually assaulted or invite lewd comments from men. In other words, women's clothing sends signals to men to hurt women. On the other hand, womanhood was also defined and policed differently outside of Anaisha's community. In Western spaces, Anaisha's "hairy arms and legs" needed to be done away with because the peer bullying she experienced signaled to her that White Western notions of femininity had no room for dark hair on one's face and body. In contrast to Anaisha, Noor (her wife) was prohibited by her family from wearing her hijab after 9/11 to protect her from the discrimination and harm they were experiencing even though she would have preferred to wear her hijab. However, Western society often views Muslim women wearing hijabs as restrictive or forced. Similar to our discussion in Chapter 3 on Western standards of beauty, these notions of what is attractive and beautiful can create a lot of pressure and threats to self-esteem for individuals who do not fit the beauty standards or who dare to defy these standards.

Outside the Confines of Heteronormativity and Tradition

For a long time, Anaisha led a double life, one within her family and the other outside of it. It was not until she was in her early 30s that her parents and siblings found out that she is queer and was dating a woman at that time. For some individuals, coming out is a choice, and for others, it is forced. The latter is what happened to Anaisha: for years, she either dodged questions about when she was ready to get married and whether she was talking to the men she was sent biodatas of, or pretended that she was dating men. She was planning to come out to her family on her own terms. Instead, she was outed because a person in her community who knew her family saw her kissing her girlfriend outside a cafe. Being outed by force is an especially jarring experience. A common assumption in Western cultures is that coming out with a nonheterosexual identity will be met with anger or rejection. Instead, Anaisha's family responded with denial, believing that she could not be queer because she was their daughter and because she was Indian. They believed that her American friends had brainwashed her. They then denied her queer identity as a "phase" that would soon pass by and continued to email biodatas to her.

At the same time, Anaisha also felt like an outsider within predominantly White queer spaces. She experienced difficulties finding other queer folks in these spaces who resonated with her experiences, who could understand why she chose to lead this double existence rather than break free of her familial ties and that her culture was still important to her even if it marginalized some of her experiences. Due to these complicated experiences, she continued to lead a double life within her community until she finally decided to tell her family she wanted to get married to Noor, a Muslim woman. These are examples of the complicated experiences that many Asian Indian Americans can experience as a result of the conflict of the influence between heteronormative and patriarchal constructs and Asian Indians with sexual minority identities.

Historical records illustrate that heterosexuality and heterosexual partnerships were not the "norm" and yet societies across the world have constructed what has been termed **compulsory heterosexuality** (Geetha, 2007). Several scholars have described this concept as not only about governing an individual's desires but also about instructing the world to only permit two types of people to exist in romantic partnership—a man and a woman (Geetha, 2007). Further, romantic partnerships should exist only monogamously. Colonial structures and policies in the Indian subcontinent ensured that heteronormativity became the legal norm with the 377 penal code described in Chapter 1, which was only recently abolished. However, scholars have also traced and connected the controlling of queer desires to the Indian caste system, as a result of its concept of endogamy.[2]

These rigid norms often have detrimental effects on Asian Indians across the gender spectrum who often grow up without an understanding of what sex or relationships are; without the freedom to openly explore their sexuality; and without knowing how to untangle a deep embedment of patriarchy that manifests through notions of consent, masculinity, and power. Oftentimes, explorations of sex and sexuality are shrouded in secrecy due to this taboo nature. For Anaisha, who grew up within the confines of rigid heteronormativity, internalized schemas about what "normal" romantic relationships and sexuality should look like became complicated experiences to combat in addition to the other bicultural identity stressors. The internalized homophobia often resulted in almost ever-present anxiety and panic attacks during her teenage years as she began to realize she was attracted to a girl in one of her classes. Anaisha felt like she could never express her inner turmoil, shame, and guilt with anyone in her family. Having grown up with no references within her community or family of individuals who identified as queer, she felt isolated in her experiences. The more that Anaisha felt that her identities fell outside of the confines of Asian Indian cultural norms, and the more apparent it became that Western LGBTQIA+ communities were mostly White-dominant spaces, the more intense her feelings of alienation became. Table 4.1 below lists some examples of questions that may come up for Asian Indians who are conflicted between their desires and the restrictions within their culture.

TABLE 4.1 Some Questions That an Asian Indian Adolescent or Young Adult Might Be Deliberating

How do you give consent? What constitutes consent?
Are my sexual needs important?
How do I regulate my sexual needs?
Can I/how do I masturbate?
What are okay sexual attitudes, beliefs, and behaviors?
How do I explore my sexuality?
What if I feel attraction to same-sex partners?
Is it normal for me to have sexual urges even when I am not in a partnership?
Is it okay for me to experiment with my sexual behaviors?
Is it shameful to talk about my sexual experiences?
Is it okay to watch porn or sexually explicit content?
How do I talk to my family about sexual identity? How do I come out to my parents?
Is it okay for me to touch my body and feel pleasure?
Is it normal for me to not want to have sex or enjoy sex?

Sexual liberation is not a task. It is not a destination that can be reached. However, it can be helpful for mental health professionals to aid Asian Indian clients in experiencing more comfort with exploring their sexuality and understanding their sexual pleasures by encouraging experimentation and autonomy while also exhibiting compassion and the ability to meet clients where they are at in their phase of identity development. The table above can be a useful guide to consider what kinds of questions Asian Indian adolescent clients might be grappling with. It is more than likely that such conversations and exploration might be very uncomfortable (for both clients and clinicians), so it is important to engage in this process with subtlety and to refrain from judgment about lack of awareness, experience, comfort, or the level of experience of your clients. It is also important to assess and check in with yourself about the comfort you have with these topics. Any discomfort you feel will manifest in your sessions with clients. The questions below can be a useful guide to consider as you begin to explore these intersectional identities with Asian Indian clients.

Clinical Questions

1. **How did you know your gender? What did your family directly or indirectly tell you about your gender?** It can be really important to understand how an individual and their family perceives gender (where they fall on the spectrum of binary gender norms).

2. **Did your family share a code of what your gender expression should entail?** This is a good question to ask because it can help a clinician understand whether there are any factors that affect body image and self-esteem.

3. **How comfortable do you feel talking about sex or sexual experiences?** As mentioned in this section, the rigid norms around sexual attitudes, behaviors, and perspectives can sometimes make it difficult for Asian Indians to feel comfortable talking about these topics, and thus it can

be useful to gauge where an Asian Indian client falls on this spectrum.

4. **Were you encouraged to explore your sexuality when you were growing up?**

5. **In what ways do you explore sexual pleasure?** While all Asian Indians experience the effects of the cultural norms around sex and sexuality, there are often deeper divides across gender. Asian Indians who identify as women may feel like it is shameful to have sexual needs, touch themselves, or experience sexual pleasure. Thus, a clinician who engages in this assessment can help an Asian Indian client feel empowered and validate their experiences.

6. **How would you describe your sexuality/sexual orientation?** This question can be modified based on the clinician's assessment of their client. For some clients, it might be helpful for the clinician to use self-disclosure by sharing their own salient cultural identities as a way to open up a conversation on intersectional identities. For example, "I identify as an Asian Indian, sexually fluid, cisgender female, and I share this because sometimes our visible and invisible identities shape our experiences and therapy relationship." This can be a helpful tool to use to increase rapport and trust with clients, but also realize that it might take a couple of sessions for Asian Indian clients to feel comfortable disclosing their identities.

Samar

Patriarchy and Bicultural Conflict

Following the pattern of the other systems of oppression described in this book, unequal dynamics of power are inherent within patriarchy. Inequalities seep into and intertwine with familial relationships. Often, Indian American families that span across both generations and international borders involve incredibly complex relational dynamics. For second-generation (and beyond) individuals like Samar—whose home base is grounded in the United States and who views India as a distant other—understanding interpersonal relationships within the family comes from deducing meaning from often indirect sources. There are two problems here: one is the stress of patriarchal oppression repeated and perpetuated within family dynamics, and the other is bicultural conflict endured by second-generation individuals who are culturally distanced from the messages they receive about family, relationships, and gender.

Many Asian Indian traditions and ways of being are lost in translation between generations of immigrants—first-generation individuals like Samar's parents are tasked with holding onto traditions (e.g., attitudes, behaviors) that feel important for their identities and well-being without the immersive environmental context in which to foster these traditional values within their own children. By the time traditions trickle down to later generations of Indian Americans, the reasons behind them may no longer be accessible. For example, Samar's parents often communicate the importance of respecting and deferring to family elders. When the extended families are able to visit one another, Samar witnesses his parents fall into the roles of attending to and placating the adults—maintaining a ruse of wealth, comfort, success, and a problem-free life—and must follow suit. His parents speak highly of their jobs despite the difficulties they face there and speak kindly of their neighbors despite hardly being friends with them; his mother wears *salwars* and serves chai. These are expectations of them—a successful life is the currency of respect for having left India; servitude is acknowledgement of the patriarchal hierarchy. Samar can deduce that there is a debt his grandparents hold over his parents, enforced through gender roles and structured power dynamics.

Not having been socialized around extended family members or to family norms outside of these infrequent and isolated visits, he perceives these practices to be inauthentic and often feels frustration, distress, and the urge to rebel. Samar also experiences confusion around his perceived hypocrisy of his parents: he knows that his parents to some extent disregarded the extended family's expectations and opinions in order to get married, and he has difficulty integrating this knowledge with their performance within family dynamics now. This can be seen as an illustration of the second-generation bicultural individual's one-step-removed experience of intergenerational or cultural trauma. There is a conflict aroused between the identities that Samar's parents hold and the value of filial piety (or *seva*)[3] they have toward their own parents. Their promotion of collectivistic family values by way of deference to and seeking approval of elders may be a reaction to familial trauma related to their intercaste marriage (deviation from cultural norms). Perhaps reinforcing patriarchal cultural norms, which give power to the extended family, is a way of making amends or healing from the rupture created by their deviation from cultural norms. However, Samar has not formed a strong enough connection with his extended family or to collectivistic cultural norms for this transaction to make sense—he would sometimes rather exclude extended family from his life altogether based on the lack of authentic community and connection he feels.

As discussed in previous chapters, there are a number of clinical implications and indicators of bicultural conflicts. With regard to navigating identity and roles within family systems, bicultural Indian Americans may experience frustration and resentment related to value conflicts, isolation, and depression from their degrees of separation from other family members, or anxiety and confusion related to an inability to feel secure in their identities.[4] It is important for clinicians to be able to note the difference between when clients are experiencing barriers to understanding the effects of patterns of intergenerational trauma versus when they are speaking to the genuine harms of patriarchal systems of oppression across cultures. The former requires insight and may lead to deep compassion, resolution of conflict, and eventual integration of identity. The latter requires a systemic approach focused on empowerment and liberation. It may not be uncommon for clients to experience distress on both individual and systemic dimensions; thus, awareness of the types of conflict and related intervention strategies are crucial for effective therapeutic work.

The Coveted Son

Another consequence of how the system of patriarchy colors Samar's familial relationships is that he is cast in the role of the coveted son. In particular, he is expected to play the coveted *American* son, which has distinct meaning in an Indian family. We described in previous chapters how being born and raised in the United States isolates Samar from the rest of his family and serves in some ways to make him feel inferior to them; however, ironically, being American is also seen as a status symbol—a symbol of privilege. In a sense, Samar's existence is representative of the success his parents are expected to achieve.

This amplifies Samar's general discomfort with identity labels and categorization, given that he rarely feels he embodies identity labels or that identity labels fully capture his experience. Samar's gender fluidity means that though he feels a masculine energy and uses masculine pronouns, he experiences gender day to day as transient. He moves between and around existing binary definitions of gender, and traditional societal expectations of gender experience and gender roles do not fit him. Although his parents have demonstrated some resistance to systems of oppression by countering casteist expectations through their intercaste marriage and certain collectivist family values by moving away from their families to the United States, they still uphold many patriarchal and cisnormative[5] values. Thus, they perceive and socialize Samar as a heterosexual man, and around them Samar's gender experience is very much internal. In order to maintain his psychological safety, he does not express gender fluidity around them.

The intersection of Samar's ethnicity and gender role expectations creates a unique set of conflicts that parallel bicultural conflicts described earlier. First, though there may be considerable overlap between gender role expectations for men in Indian and Western societies, there can also be differences related to context. For example, independence in an Asian Indian collectivistic culture may be valued as an important characteristic for a man to be a stable anchor for his family of origin to lean on, whereas in Western individualistic culture it may be related to his ability to securely move beyond his family of origin. Living in the United States, Samar is exposed to both collectivistic and individualistic foundations of gender role expectations and must integrate the two (Figure 4.1a). The second conflict involves Samar's generational status as a second-generation immigrant—rather than integrating two separate frameworks of gender role expectations, Samar may grapple with the creation of a third framework (Figure 4.1b). There is a unique pressure on Samar as an American natural citizen to be successful and to have an active role in establishing his family's roots in the United States. We described in Chapter 3 how Samar's parents may socialize him, explicitly or implicitly, to value certain career paths over others; this can also be reflective of gender norms and the expectation that men will pursue prestigious, well-paid, and sustainable careers. Further, Samar bears the burden of making up for the ways in which his parents digressed from the systems of oppression that govern them; he is in some ways their apology to their families, communicated through their pride in him and his accomplishments during visits from extended family. With this responsibility comes an implication that there would be a certain level of disappointment if he were a woman, an implication that his status as a man in the eyes of his family gives him a privilege and an honor he would not otherwise have. Thus, the fact that Samar does not identify as a man is an added layer of complexity and source of psychological pain, compounding the oppression from patriarchal systems he experiences.

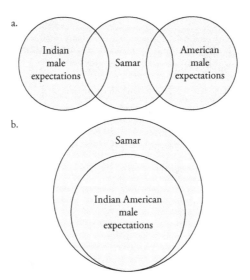

FIGURE 4.1   Bicultural Gender Role Expectations

Note: Samar's gender identity is fluid. He does not identify as male; however, he is perceived and socialized as male by his family and by society. Thus, Samar experiences the conflicts and pressures associated both with being upheld as a son in his Indian American household and with his gender fluidity.

Failure to match expectations comes with the risk of being (or feeling) devalued and losing a sense of identity as Samar navigates roles within his family and communities. There may be added distress reflecting the erasure of Samar's genderfluid identity by his family and the gender expectations placed upon him. Clinical work addressing the mental health consequences of the system of patriarchy should be mindful of the ways in which Indian and Western communities imply binary gender expectations, as well as of intersectionality with generational status and intergenerational cultural traumas.

Clinical Questions

1. **What are some messages you received throughout your childhood about gender roles and masculinity?** Asking about masculinity instead of about male gender roles is important for affirming Samar's experience of gender.

(Continued)

This question may help elucidate sources of pressure and socialization that are most salient.

2. **Where (and with whom) do you express your gender, and where do you restrict your gender expression? Why?** These questions can help to highlight facilitators and barriers to Samar's gender expression.

3. **Are there spaces in your life where you feel safe and comfortable completely being yourself?** A positive psychology and strengths-based approach, this question encourages exploration of positive experiences to make them more salient, to acknowledge them in contrast to the more difficult experiences that may be more naturally discussed in therapy, and to understand what makes these spaces feel safe for Samar.

4. **What is it like for you when your extended family visits?** A question that is open-ended and nondirective such as this allows for exploration of potentially complex experiences without inadvertently limiting them.

5. **What is it like to navigate gender role expectations as the U.S.-born person in your family?** The intention of this question is to explore Samar's experiences at the intersection of his identities as a second-generation immigrant, genderfluid person who was socialized as male. It may be beneficial with some more psychologically minded clients to name and describe intersectionality when assessing their experiences.

5

Threading Together

Gaps in Current Training Programs

There are several psychology and social work graduate programs that aim to provide their graduate students with a strong foundation in understanding systemic oppression. Regardless of whether these programs incorporate a lens of liberation psychology, critical race theory, intersectionality, or other such theories, these frameworks are often taught in institutional settings or programmatic structures that maintain and perpetuate White supremacist norms, making it difficult for students to gain a meaningful understanding of how to bridge these knowledge bases with their therapy approaches. While the social work field is more advanced in its incorporation of social justice and advocacy values into its code of ethics, social work programs are still taught in institutions that uphold White supremacist values.

Aside from intellectual conceptualization, many therapeutic approaches lack concrete methods, skills, and ways of thinking that mental health professionals can use to engage in liberatory practices that truly bridge their understanding of systemic oppression with a cultural healing framework. For instance, rarely are graduate students in these fields taught and encouraged to embrace their own healing journeys that involve deepening their connection with their ancestral histories and engaging in healing practices that include their own cultural traditions (beyond the recommendation of scheduling their own therapy services).

When we think about this more deeply, it is bewildering to grasp that while the objective of such programs is to educate students about the histories of systemic oppression and marginalization of various minoritized communities, it does so in the same systemic structures that perpetuate these White supremacist norms. Instead, White supremacy cultural norms of burn out, perfectionism, urgency, paternalism, fear of open conflict, individualism, and quantity over quality (Tatum, 1997) are often embodied as programmatic structures even in programs that aim to teach students the importance of dismantling systemic oppression. For instance, some graduate programs may educate their students about White supremacist cultural norms and yet the same characteristics are often experienced by graduate students enrolled in these training programs. It is quite common for graduate students in general as well as in mental health training programs to feel burned out, bogged down by perfectionistic tendencies when working on their thesis or dissertations, and other such dominant norms that contradict what a true dismantling systemic oppression program would look like.

We believe that we have to begin with ourselves, and with our own healing, in order to provide culturally inclusive therapy services. In order for clinicians to engage in liberatory practices in their work with Asian Indian American clients—as well as other communities of Color in clinical settings—it is essential to first begin with how the clinicians themselves are engaging in practices that prioritize their own healing in order to engage and facilitate the healing journeys of their clients. When we talk about healing, we refer to both psychoemotional concerns and ancestral traumas. In this chapter, we will explore two major themes: (a) how traditional therapeutic frameworks reproduce White supremacist oppression and fall short of liberatory ideology, and (b) what we can do instead to break out of the restrictive bonds of these frameworks. We will explore a little about the origins of psychotherapy, how it has evolved to repeat problematic patterns, and how we can move away from these problematic patterns.

Therapy Is Good, Right? Origins of and Problems With Traditional Frameworks

As we introduced in Chapter 1, psychology as we know it today is grounded in a bias toward normalizing the privileged, White—and often heterosexual, cisgender male—experience, which other scholars have described as "WEIRD" (Henrich et al., 2010).[1] Such a heavy focus on normalizing the WEIRD experience in our field has led clinicians to falter when asked to center other identities in our work. We as a society are better at conceptualizing mental health problems and well-being for the WEIRD population than we are nearly anyone else who falls outside of those identity categories. Our treatments, then, are also naturally tailored to fit the population that we are best at conceptualizing. It is of note that how we think about psychotherapy has expanded and changed over time; however, patterns of reproducing oppression have been present from the beginning.

In part because of the tumultuous historical time in which psychotherapy emerged as a field, it is difficult to ascertain a common understanding of what "traditional" frameworks of psychotherapy entail. For example, the founders of some of the first psychotherapies (e.g., Sigmund Freud, Viktor Frankl, and Alfred Adler) were Jewish. Many foundational psychoanalytic beliefs stem from Judaism, but there was fear that psychoanalysis would not be accepted in the anti-Semitic society of Europe at the time (Johansson & Punzi, 2019; Kuriloff, 2014). Psychoanalysts fled Europe and practiced and developed the field in exile, finding ways to separate psychoanalysis from their Jewish beliefs. Freud was known for pushing psychoanalysis as a science that would be digestible by the oppressive majority, which meant he was under a lot of pressure to prove its validity outside of what was a derogatory concept of "Jewish science" (Johansson & Punzi, 2019, p. 140). Often, the way to "validate" psychoanalysis—and this pattern is seen today—was to associate it with medical science, which was more accepted and understood by mainstream society. From the beginning, a definition of science that was already poised to oppress others was used as a way to squash what psychotherapy otherwise could have been.

Although psychoanalysis is what is commonly thought of as "traditional" psychotherapy because it is one of the oldest frameworks known to the Western world, it is notable that the versions of it that are taught and practiced in the United States are psychodynamic therapies, which are more conducive to connections to biologically based sciences, the scientific method, and incorporation into other therapies. This trend toward "science" (and the restricted definition of what science is) has been mirrored in psychotherapy training, where researchers have found that faculty members in the United States tend to favor a cognitive-behavioral orientation over others and have noted concerns that "we may inadvertently be training a generation of students who equate a particular orientation with 'good science' and, by implication, other orientations for which compelling data in fact exist, with 'bad science' or 'no science'" (Heatherington et al., 2013, p. 369).

The American Psychological Association outlines five main therapeutic orientations: psychoanalysis/psychodynamic, behavior, cognitive, humanistic, and integrative/holistic; however, there are numerous subfields, offshoots, and modified frameworks. A number of the frameworks that exist today emerged out of recognition of the ways in which existing therapies did not feel applicable or appropriate for given (often non-WEIRD) populations.

Of the two themes outlined in our introduction to this chapter, these new frameworks have acknowledged the first: traditional therapeutic frameworks are born from oppressive science and therefore also reproduce oppression (Duran et al., 2008). New therapeutic frameworks are labeled "multicultural counseling" or described as efforts to move toward multicultural competence. Unfortunately, the reality of multicultural counseling is that for the most part it is simply an extension of Western/traditional frameworks—thus, born still of the same oppressive science. While it is beyond the scope of this book to describe these endeavors in detail, there is a substantial body of research attempting to adapt Western models of therapy for marginalized populations in the name of multicultural competence.

There is also a body of work aiming to validate nontraditional therapy frameworks by associating them with or testing them along Western ideologies. For example, mindfulness-based approaches and yoga are examples of healing practices that were not considered seriously until they were appropriated—now, it is in most cases illegal to use these healing practices professionally without licensure as a yoga therapy practitioner under the guidelines of Western organizations. Thus, there has been an ebb and flow in how therapy has evolved; it has even been redefined at times in efforts to mitigate oppression but has still remained trapped within oppressive ideologies.

Colonialism

Decades ago, scholars like Frantz Fanon wrote about the ways in which colonialism leaves scars on and in the body, that the true cause of psychological problems is colonialism, and that the only true way to treat psychological problems is to work for the liberation of colonized people. Fanon thought it was both unethical and not possible to name colonial problems—political and systemic issues—as individual-level mental health problems and to attempt to treat them as such (Burman, 2020). Therapists who align with Fanon's conceptualization of mental health believe that colonialism has a direct psychic effect. Specifically, we believe the cycle of power and oppression that represents colonialism is internalized, and creates conflict between people (those with power and those without power) and within people (the parts of the self that resemble the oppressor and the characteristics that are targets of oppression).[2] Based on this line of thinking, we believe that Western/traditional models of therapy can function as a type of colonialism that at best do not address the true roots of psychological problems, and at worst repeat colonialist power patterns that perpetuate harm against marginalized people.

Many minoritized communities view conventional Western clinical approaches as dangerous. For instance, studies with Indigenous people in the North America show that Western clinical approaches are akin to ethnic cleansing and faith conversion (Gone, 2008). Research from other colonized countries describes Eurocentric counseling practices as oppressive because of their assumption that Indigenous knowledge is unscientific. The use of these approaches deprives people of learning from their centuries-old ways of knowing in favor of imposed and prescribed Eurocentric value structures. As we discussed earlier, even Western models that aim or claim to embrace cross-cultural competency are restricted only to certain ways of knowing that follow the "rules of the academy," or what is considered to be scientific and rigorous in the eyes of privileged, powerful people. This is not liberation or decolonization—it is neocolonialism or repackaged colonialism.

As a result of multitiered systems of inequality, as illustrated throughout the book, many Asian Indians have been conditioned to adopt fragments of themselves, those of which fit the colonized worldview and of half knowledge. Many Asian Indian Americans (especially children and adolescents) may not be familiar with their own ancestral histories, traditions, and practices but are impacted by the intergenerational course and relationships that have influenced their upbringing and livelihood. For example, if Asian Indian American adolescents are asked about their caste background or the origins of their families' traditions, many may say they do not know or not be able to provide much depth. This is true of many communities. As a result of colonization, war-torn regions, migrations, and complex intergenerational trauma histories, many of us are fragmented as Western society, and in turn White supremacy, often focuses on the individual, on the compartmentalized selves versus the whole community and collective histories that often shape who we are. Thus, when we think about liberation from Western frameworks, it is in this context of how we view individuals (and communities) as a collective, with both pain and healing intertwined.

The Role of the Clinician

Psychotherapy that addresses the colonial, oppressive roots of psychopathology is both anticolonial and decolonial. This means that not only is the work against colonialism, but it also operates outside of oppressive frameworks (such as those described in the previous section) and heals through dismantling and breaking free from oppressive frameworks. As clinicians, in order to heed calls for decolonizing psychotherapy, we need to acknowledge what has thus far kept us trapped in a cycle of reproducing oppression for marginalized populations by practicing therapy within Western frameworks. Psychotherapist Dick Blackwell has spoken about how there is an element of guilt involved for the privileged party in a dynamic relationship; when the more powerful party in a dyad is cognizant of the history of colonialism and sensitive to the harm perpetuated by power imbalances, they experience guilt related to their position in the dyad. This guilt presents a barrier to working toward true equalization of people and power. "It's hard to be equal with people who make us feel guilty," Blackwell says; "the most common defense against all this particularly in the psychotherapeutic community is simply to ignore it" (Blackwell, 2003, p. 457).

To work through this, it is important to remain mindful of where the guilt is coming from: our clients are not the sources of our discomfort. In fact, our clients themselves probably experience a counterpart to our guilt—perhaps shame, anger, resentment, or a myriad of other appropriate feelings of distress. Power inequalities are not inherently tied to privilege and marginalization; it is because of colonialism that power dynamics reproduce cycles of oppression. Rather than taking in our clients' pain as if our power puts us in a position of opposition, it is our job as clinicians to work with our clients collaboratively to create healing.

Creating healing is difficult, if not impossible, without proper and accurate understanding of clients' problems. A consequence of how psychotherapy is conceptualized and taught in the United States is that therapists are often unaware of life experiences that fall outside of the bounds of Western ideology (Duran & Duran, 2000). In other words, life experiences that cannot be understood through the lens of a predefined scientific construct often do not even breach therapists' conscious awareness, creating a divide between therapists and clients of many marginalized communities. This problem is addressed by using resources such as this one to increase diversity in how we think about life, which in turn leads us to ask better questions and practice appropriate ways of healing.

Philosophies of Suffering and Healing

We believe it is somewhat superficial to call for a change in how clinicians conceptualize and treat mental health problems with marginalized populations like Asian Indians without also asking you to reflect on your own philosophies of healing and suffering. Without knowing what you believe, adopting new philosophies can be more like putting a Band-Aid over the problems and gaps in Western thinking that we have described, rather than truly expanding your understanding of people. Further, people across different cultures often conceptualize mental health and suffering in ways which may be different from how Western practitioners view suffering and mental health. Thus, it is essential to be cognizant of how your own perspective differs from that of your clients. In the previous chapters, we covered how Asian Indians in the United States are impacted by three different systems of inequality; we then illustrated why and how Western models of therapy are insufficient and often harmful in addressing their mental health concerns. Before the next section about appropriate ways to approach healing with Asian Indians, we ask that you take a moment to integrate your thoughts. Figure 5.1 offers a flowchart to help you with this process. As you complete this exercise, try to be mindful of the language, terminology, and conceptualization differences regarding mental health across cultures. In particular, we encourage you to be mindful of your own biases in how you think about mental health: be curious about what comes to mind when you think about mental health. For example, we described in Chapter 1 how Western psychology is only beginning to become aware of and understand different presentations of mental health difficulties, including somatic (physical) experiences. How do somatic experiences play into your conceptualization of mental health? Furthermore, how else might you think about mental health and suffering that we have not explicitly named?

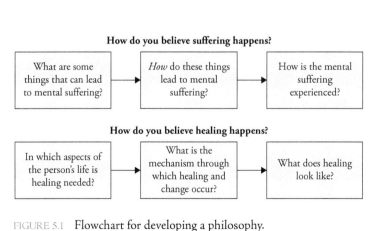

FIGURE 5.1 Flowchart for developing a philosophy.

Guidelines for Clinicians

Moving Away From Deficit Model (Diagnose and Fix Model)

Mental health professionals are often provided with an extensive educational foundation with regard to psychopathology and diagnostic frameworks during their graduate training programs, which allows them to assign diagnoses to their clients who fit within certain categories of symptoms. The diagnostic framework can be useful to conceptualize some of the mental health concerns an individual is experiencing as well as aid in the formulation of a treatment plan. A downside to the sole focus on diagnosis is that it can often result in a hyper focus on symptoms rather than humanity, with the objective of "fixing" symptoms. Even disciplines that have a strengths-based foundation, such as social work, still operate within a system that upholds this diagnose and fix model, forcing them to rely to an extent on diagnosing psychopathology. This reductionist view not only limits clinicians from looking at their clients more holistically, but also creates an enormous amount of pressure on them to "save" their clients from their mental health crisis. For some clinicians, this can lead to the development of a savior complex and the perpetuation of a power dynamic that ultimately serves to maintain social distance between clinicians and their clients. While the intention behind the savior complex often emerges from a good place, it can prevent clinicians from truly understanding their clients by exploring the ways they have survived thus far and all the other elements that make up who they are. For clinicians whose training was not grounded in strengths-based philosophy, it can also prevent them from empowering their clients by creating a doctor-patient dynamic in which clients are always help seekers and clinicians are always help providers. Finally, the pressure clinicians experience can feel like a burden to resolve all the trauma and emotional suffering that clients present with; given the overlapping systems of inequality discussed throughout the book and all of their implications, it is unsurprising that Asian Indian clients would experience patterns of resurfacing symptoms due to the complexities of their experiences paired with intergenerational traumas. Therapies focused only on symptoms and diagnoses would easily become tiresome while simultaneously underserving Asian Indian clients.

We understand that diagnoses are often needed from a systemic perspective on service provision—given that the United States is, ultimately, a Western society—due to the requirements of insurance companies. That being said, here is a thought exercise: Imagine if the aim of the initial few sessions of psychotherapy was not on assessing clients for diagnoses but rather on listening deeply to their stories and exploring their ancestral histories. Rather than focusing solely on their current challenges, imagine if we also dove deeper into our clients' own and their families' survival strategies. To draw a succinct parallel to Chapter 1, imagine if we asked better questions. How might our treatment plans change? What might we learn about our clients that we cannot learn from a diagnostically focused framework, and how might this knowledge help us to create more appropriate and meaningful work with them? This is not to say that an objective of therapy should not be to support and help clients understand and resolve their challenges; however, we believe it would be a disservice to both clients and clinicians for this to be the sole focus.

Connecting With Ancestral Roots

One of the most detrimental aspects of the ongoing colonization process is that there has been a generational shedding of cultural identities, values, traditions, and ways of knowing and living in people. Liberating from Western frameworks means shifting away from the internalization of Western norms and standards and beginning to adopt a both-and approach (e.g., using both Western talk therapy and cultural healing practices). In Chapter 1, we described how human beings desire to feel grounded and rooted in their communities, like trees. But when the community is hostile in ways that require us to shed parts of ourselves rather than allowing us to establish roots, how can we work toward this goal? This is where the healing practice of connecting with ancestral roots comes in. Internalization of Western ideology can make us forget the roots we do have: the histories and stories of our ancestors. Connecting with ancestral roots is regaining knowledge that was erased by colonization.

An aspect of colonization involves renouncing all that does not fit the colonizer's worldview. In everyday life experiences, as you read throughout the presented case examples, this can manifest as experiences of bullying, ostracization, and being made to feel different or inferior. These experiences might lead Asian Indian Americans to learn from a young age that their family traditions or cultural practices are not accepted or "normal" within American spaces. For example, Asian Indian adolescents may not want to bring homemade Indian food to school ("it is smelly") or attend school with their hair oiled with coconut oil ("it is dirty") as a result of feeling negatively evaluated or experiencing bullying from their school peers or administrative staff. Healing may come from helping clients to connect with their lost or rejected traditional practices to their ancestral roots: the individual-level shame that underlies clients' rejection of their cultural traditions can be shifted to community-level security when ancestors and histories are acknowledged. The sense of inferiority felt at the individual level can be shifted to negative associations toward the appropriate target: colonization.

As clinicians, we must also keep in mind that while ancestral connection and knowledge is important, it is not about idealization or idolizing our ancestors. Rather, ancestral connection is about helping clients gain and regain knowledge about their histories and where they come from, about the oppressive and privileged systems they experience or have inherited, and about intergenerational resilience, cultural healing practices, and celebrational rituals. The idea behind connecting with ancestral roots is that knowing fuller stories will enable clients to feel more empowered and rooted, even in the midst of the storm they experience.

One tangible way to begin the liberation process outside of simply understanding why it is needed is by learning more about our own histories, migration stories, and ancestors. In working with clients, it is integral for clinicians to listen for intergenerational practices that clients may have heard about from family members in childhood and have since denounced or forgotten about; the best way to develop a good listening ear for these is to practice the process with yourself, by getting in touch with your own ancestral roots.

Ancient Asian Indian Healing Traditions

The Indian subcontinent is home to a people who have practiced a range of ancient healing traditions and medicine that date back thousands of years. Ancient Asian Indian healing traditions (used to treat a range of diseases and ailments) are informed through cultural values, norms, beliefs, and worldviews. These healing practices include *Mishing* practices (medicinal practices originating from Northeastern Indian regions), *Siddha* medicine (ancient Dravidian medicine (10000–4000 BCE) that originated in Southern India), *Ayurvedic* medicine (encompass living, dietary, and spiritual prescriptions), *Unani* (Islamic medical tradition), *Sowa-Rig-Pa* (use of herbs, animal products, water, and mystical power in treatments), *Dervish* (healers who use religious and cultural practices to treat mental health concerns), *Moalj belkoran* (male-identified healers who use Islamic scriptures to safeguard against negative forces or evil spirits), astrology or palm reading, **sound meditation**, poison therapy, naturopathy, and energy healing, as well as old and modern yoga practices (Al-Krenawi & Graham, 2000; AlRawi, 2011; Dalal, 2007; Gupta et al., 2014; Kakar, 1982). Some of these healing traditions incorporate folk dances, songs, folklore, poetry, or meditation in their healing ceremonies (Dalal, 2007). Ancient healing practices reflect the collective and amassed wisdom of Asian Indian societies' lived experiences and knowledge base of healing and wounding (Dalal, 2007; Kakar, 1982).

Ancient healing traditions also focus on the role of the *sacred*. "Sacred" in this context refers to God, deities, demons, enlightened spiritual human beings, natural elements, or spirits of ancestors that represent the specific religious beliefs or cultural practices of both the healer and the patient (Dalal, 2007; Kakar, 1982). These religious beliefs or cultural practices almost always involve a legend or story associated with the type of healing tradition, which is why there is often reference to specific metaphysical beings in these sessions. Therefore, within these healing sessions, the healer might focus on channeling the psychic energies within and outside of the patient in order to alleviate the ailment for which the patient has sought help (Dalal, 2007; Kakar, 1982). The healer might repeat sacred verses, engage in purification rituals, prepare sacred talismans with protective energies, or use herbs or oils to aid the healing of the patient (Kumar et al., 2005). Further, there is a central focus on the interdependence of the mind-body-spirit, emerging out of beliefs that healing occurs when all of these interconnected systems are in harmony. In this framework, the patient is not alone but a part of a larger ancestral community that has shaped and influenced their livelihood. Thus, healers may invite the patient's ancestors into the healing space by reciting their names, or placing pictures or ancestral objects in the room. Unlike Western therapy sessions, traditional healing sessions can also occur in front of family or community members.

Western psychological frameworks often fail to account for the spiritual and somatic interconnections with the mind and body, and in this way are limited in being able to provide true holistic healing. Traditional healing can further depart from Western practices in that the power of the healing ceremony is often associated with the story of the healer or the healing space rather than just the individual patient (Dalal, 2007). In this way, the healer themselves becomes a powerful source of the healing work rather than being a neutral spectator of the experience.

It is imperative to note that Asian Indian healing traditions differ based on the religious and cultural practices of specific communities. While there can be many distinctions among various Asian Indian communities' healing traditions, there can be significant overlap (e.g., role of the sacred, dietary and herb prescriptions), and members of different communities may seek healers that do not practice their religion or cultural traditions. For instance, it is common for both Muslim and non-Muslim Indians to go to **dargahs** and **Sufi masters** for different ailments.

Other differences in healing traditions practiced by Asian Indians are related to accessibility related to identities such as caste. Some ancient Asian Indian medicinal traditions such as Ayurveda and **Siddha medicine** were often limited to upper-caste people (e.g., both the Ayurvedic practitioners and patients are often of upper-caste status), but many other healing methods have long been practiced by a range of folk healers and Indian indigenous people, often referred to as **adivasis** (Panghal et al., 2010). Many adivasi communities use their extensive knowledge of medicinal plants and herbs to treat diseases and improve overall health and well-being (Panghal et al., 2010).[3] As one can see, the range of healing traditions practiced by Asian Indians is immense, which is why the suggested readings at the end of this book will be helpful.

Preferences for and Engagement With Healing

Asian Indians may have complicated experiences of relating to or wanting to connect with their ancestral healing practices. For many Asian Indians, their ancestral wisdom and knowledge has trickled down in bits and pieces, and some of it is lost in their present awareness. For others, these ancient traditions are sacred and sought when they need healing. And for still others, these healing traditions might be painful reminders of traumatic experiences or misunderstood mental illness or life challenges. For example, Asian Indians may be forcibly taken to traditional healers to cure something that does not need to be cured (e.g., gender identity, sexual orientation, sexual choices) or individuals with mental illnesses might be forced to receive traditional healing against their will. The key here with the "treating" of mental illness in this manner is that it is against the will of the person. As with nearly everything else, the act of seeking psychological healing services manifests on a spectrum: Asian Indians living in the United States may seek traditional healers to varying degrees based on their level of indoctrination of Western medicine, heritage cultural awareness, and ancestral or individual history with these traditional healing practices.

A consequence of colonial brainwashing by way of framing Western traditions as "acceptable" and non-Western traditions as "unacceptable" is that many Asian Indians now prefer Western medicine and view it as the best or only option. In some ways this may not read immediately as a problem; for example, it suggests that Asian Indians are open to healing, which some clinicians correctly identify as progress in breaking through stigma against mental health help-seeking behaviors. However, a preference for Western medicine can also be harmful as it perpetuates harmful ideologies regarding the inferiority of other ways of healing/being/knowing and maintains colonial systems of inequality. We are cognizant that by introducing liberatory practices as the knowledge of how to properly ask questions, prompt exploration, and empower clients, we are still in the realm of Western talk therapy. Thus, it is important to recognize that this practice is only the beginning of liberation: asking the right questions is the necessary bridge to move away from oppressive Western frameworks. We can help clients to frame colonialism as the appropriate underlying mechanism of hardship and encourage them to connect to their ancestral roots, but this happens through talk therapy. It is entirely possible, then, that through this process clients will move away from us (e.g., away from Western healing practices like talk therapy itself) and toward ancestral healing methods practiced by members of their own communities. We as clinicians need to be open to this possibility. For example, a clinician could give a homework assignment to their client to learn about what their ancestors did when they were in pain or needed healing, or what their ancestors believed about healing in general.[4] The objective of such a task is not to force Asian Indian clients to limit themselves to only engage in healing practices from their own cultural traditions but rather to open up their world of forgotten medicine, which in of itself can be a powerful healing tool. The choice, then, to pursue either exclusively their own cultural healing practices, both Western talk therapy and their own heritage traditions, or Western talk therapy alone is up to the client to determine. This allows clinicians to have a range of options to offer Asian Indian clients when discussing their treatment and also permits an expansion of healing services rather than an exclusively Western approach.

Nuanced Framework of Boundaries and Families

A distinctly Western and individualistic approach to understanding human functioning that we have noticed in therapeutic practice and training is how to handle "toxic" families. Often upon hearing the complex and layered difficulties Asian Indians experience with navigating systems of inequality as individuals and within family units, Western clinicians may feel pulled to conceptualize the family as a problem. Now, this is true for some, and Asian Indians certainly may decide to disconnect or detach from their own families due to a variety of reasons (such as lack of acceptance of sexual identity, interracial or interreligious marriages, or resistance to traditional norms of marriage and procreation). However, many Asian Indians may not prefer or even want this option. Rather, they may feel judged or rejected by therapists who attempt to discourage or push them toward breaking ties with their family members. Regarding retention of Asian Indian clients in therapy, this could be a barrier for clients to feel comfortable returning to sessions. Ironically, this may be especially true for Asian Indian clients who were raised in strict families wherein family members have tried to impose all of their decisions on them. A therapist trying to impose their judgments on them may actually be recreating the same dynamics. Thus, rather than conceptualizing clients' decisions to remain in their current family dynamics as problematic, it may be more therapeutic to help them explore how they might survive in their current family relationships.

A related concept is the Western conceptualization of boundaries. Western norms around boundaries often tend to be rigid and embedded within individualistic ideals, and this often manifests in the way Western practitioners diagnose mental illnesses or assess psychopathology. In other words, Western clinicians may diagnose psychopathology for clients where there is none because they are assessing boundaries and relationships through the lens of Western ideologies. Frequently, communities of Color whose familial and community relationships involve collective decision-making and close family relationships may be inaccurately viewed as enmeshed or dysfunctional. We caution against overgeneralization and acknowledge that ongoing harm may occur in family settings, especially within families who share different intersecting identities or trauma histories. We simply suggest that clinicians maintain awareness of their proneness to painting clients with the same broad stroke of pathology in terms of relationships rather than viewing each dynamic as unique—a problem unfortunately perpetuated by clinical tools such as the *DSM*.

Authentic Experiencing

Imagine if clients who do not feel safe to fully be themselves were empowered to experience their lives authentically. A major consequence of colonization, associated with all of the ways of disconnection from ancestral roots described earlier, is that colonized people become restricted in their ways of being. Societal codes of conduct reinforce colonial ideologies and label certain ways of being as unacceptable, abnormal, or inferior; in other words, they reinforce hierarchies. Under this framework, it can feel—and, in some ways, truly be—unsafe for marginalized individuals to be their authentic selves. A person's own true experiences, desires, and drives can be overshadowed

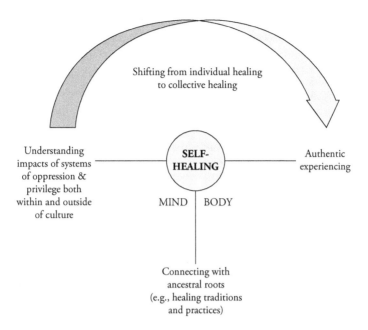

Shifting from individual healing
to collective healing

Understanding
impacts of systems
of oppression &
privilege both
within and outside
of culture

**SELF-
HEALING**

Authentic
experiencing

MIND | BODY

Connecting with
ancestral roots
(e.g., healing traditions
and practices)

FIGURE 5.2   Illustration of a liberatory process in therapy.

by what society and their families expect of them. When this happens, the effects can be felt even on a micro, everyday level wherein individuals bring fragmented components of themselves rather than their full selves. For example, a person who feels unsafe being their authentic self in society may have trouble within a therapeutic setting identifying their own real thoughts and expressing their emotions. They may feel uncomfortable focusing on themselves because they may not have been allowed to or had the space to do so before. They may not know what unobstructed agency feels like, or what freedom feels like. Authenticity may feel unfamiliar to them. Therapists are in a unique position to help such clients practice authentic experiencing— that is, clinicians can work to create safety within the therapeutic space for clients to practice getting to know their true selves without fear of judgment or retribution. This is less a method and more so a goal of liberatory healing: authentic experiencing can be thought of as a tangible mechanism of freedom or liberation.

Authentic experiencing can often be difficult because it also refers to understanding how an individual is connected, in the collective sense, with their ancestors and cultural practices. Figure 5.2 illustrates the process that clinicians who begin to adopt a more liberatory perspective might use when conceptualizing healing work with their clients. Note that the process also involves healing on the part of the clinician in order to be effective. The idea is that a true healing process involves bridging the mind (understanding of systemic inequalities) and the body (authentic experiencing) via connecting with one's ancestral roots and cultural practices. The act of bridging involves a shift from individual to collective healing. This emerges from popular forms of Western talk therapies focusing on the mind rather than somatic and spirit experiencing strategies.

Summary

We are in a period of critical transformation that is calling for the shedding of old, oppressive systems to make room for a more expansive mental health framework. What this means for the mental health field is that clinicians are tasked with unlearning old-world ideologies and internalized oppressive structures that promote separation, individualism, and bias in order to support clients in more holistic ways. This unlearning process is crucial because unlearning requires healing intergenerational sociocultural wounds of both the therapist and client. Throughout this book, we have aimed to provide a framework to describe how three primary systems of inequality create barriers for Asian Indian Americans in navigating society freely as their authentic cultural selves. We hope that this framework will be useful for clinicians to consider when working with Asian Indian clients in the United States.

Glossary

Acculturation: A type of adjustment process that is said to occur when an individual or groups of people from a different heritage culture come into first-hand contact with another group of people who practice a different culture. Acculturation is often defined in terms of immigrants arriving into a new country with a Eurocentric majority culture and the sociocultural and psychological adaptation process that tends to occur as a result of navigating two different cultural worlds.

Adivasi: Indian people who are considered indigenous to the Indian subcontinent.

Assimilation: The process of adopting Eurocentric or U.S.-dominant cultural norms and rejecting one's own traditional culture and practices to cope with the tension of navigating two different cultural worlds.

Ayurvedic Medicine: An ancient form of medicine that stems from the Vedic culture and was taught for thousands of years in an oral tradition from accomplished masters to their disciples. It focuses on prevention and physical health through prescription of lifestyle practices (e.g., dietary changes, yoga, massage, and meditation) and changing thinking patterns. According to Ayurvedic scriptures, natural elements (air, fire, earth, water, and space) integrate into the body and are divided into three components. Issues with either of these three components can cause physical or emotional ailments that are then treated by dietary or lifestyle changes.

Biodata: Usually a 1-page document that includes information on physical characteristics (e.g., height, weight, skin tone), pictures, occupational and educational information, and family background (parent's name, location, caste, geographical region) used for matchmaking purposes.

Bollywood: Akin to Hollywood in India; the name of the movie industry that produces movies in the Hindi language. However, Bollywood, while the largest and most popular movie industry in India, is one of many movie industries. There are many movie industries in India based on geographical region and language (e.g., Tollywood [Bengali-language movies], South India cinema, Malayalam movies).

Caste: Fixed assigned categories used to differentiate among groups of people, with Brahmins (priests) at the top of the system and Shudras (household help, latrine workers) at the bottom of the system. Caste has and continues to be used as a basis for discrimination both in India and in the United States.

Collectivistic (cultures): Cultures that emphasize values around group cohesion and harmony in decision-making and interactions. People from collectivistic cultures tend to perceive the community as higher than any one individual.

Colorism: Differentiation based on an individual's skin color whereby those with lighter skin tones are seen as more intelligent and attractive and those with darker skin tones are viewed as less attractive, hard-working, or intelligent, which often influence matrimonial and hiring decisions.

Compulsory Heterosexuality: Cultural conditioning that dictates that relationships should exist monogamously and only within heterosexual partnerships.

Dalit: An identity label that individuals and communities who have experienced oppression as a result of the Indian caste system have used to reclaim their identity and has become part of resistance and liberatory movements.

Dargah: This is a sacred place where a shrine is built over the grave of a respected/admired religious figure who prayed or meditated at this site. These figures are usually Sufi masters or Dervish.

Dervish: Healers who are devoted followers of Islamic Sufism who use religious and cultural practices to treat mental health concerns. Dervish perform mystical Sufi ceremonies called *Sema* where they engage in whirling rituals that often leaves them and the audience in a state of nirvana.

Desi: A term that many Asian Indians may use to refer to themselves as from the Indian/South Asian diaspora.

Enculturation: This refers to the socialization process toward one's own indigenous and ancestral practices, values, and ideas.

Endogamy: The custom of marrying within caste or subcaste, class, or religion.

Evil Eye: This is a common superstitious belief in a curse being cast by an evil glare as a reason for difficult circumstances or ailments. As a result, many Asian Indians might engage in certain rituals or wear certain ornaments to protect themselves from this evil eye.

Fakir: Fakir are Muslim medicine people.

Generational Status: Often referred to as the generational level of an immigrant. The following can be helpful markers: (a) first-generation (immigrant) individuals in the United States are those born and raised outside of the United States whose parents were also born and raised in another country, (b) 1.5 generation individuals are those who immigrated to the United States as children or as adolescents, (c) second generation individuals are born and raised in the United States, with one or both parents born outside of the United States, and (d) third generation and above generations refer to individuals who are born and raised in the United States as were their parents and their grandparents, or their great-grandparents, immigrated to the United States.

Harijan: This is another identity label used by lower-caste or caste-oppressed communities within Hinduism.

Hijra: Biological males who reject biological masculine identity and identify either as women, or not men, or in-between man and woman, or neither man nor woman.

Homeopathy: This Western healing tradition emerged in India fairly recently. It focuses on the body's natural capacity to heal itself.

Identity Diffusion: A concept that has emerged out of adolescent identity development literature as a result of adolescents not being able to integrate or commit to identities due to a variety of factors. Adolescents can experience identity diffusion when there are difficulties with integrating self-concept with self and in relationship with others. In the context of this book, identity diffusion may occur when Asian Indians have difficulties establishing a sense of identity when they experience a variety of pushes and pulls in different directions due to bicultural identity conflicts.

Individualistic (Cultures): Cultures that center the self and immediate families, with a focus on independence in decision-making, lifestyle, and personal growth.

Joint Families: Types of families that often consist of two or more generations of families residing together.

Kinnar: A term that many Asian Indian transgender and intersex people use to identify themselves.

Marginalization: The experience of being decentered and abnormalized (i.e., pushed to the margins). Describes both being disadvantaged and experiencing barriers against achieving success and comfort in life based on having certain identities.

Mishing: Indigenous Indian community that inhabit parts of the Northeastern regions of India.

Model Minority Myth: Describing Asian Americans and Asian subgroups, the myth is that they are naturally hardworking, intelligent, and successful despite the hardships associated with immigration and being a racial minority in the United States. The myth is often used to oppress other racial minorities by upholding Asians as an example of how minorities can or should be successful in the face of hardship. This perpetuates systemic oppression, divides racial minorities, and minimizes discrimination faced by Asians.

Multicultural Competence: Having the knowledge and the skills necessary to embrace cultural diversity and to engage effectively and appropriately with people across cultures.

Naturotherapy: Natural healing method that stems from the belief that toxins accumulate in the human body and is the cause of diseases. Focuses on the use of the healing powers of nature rather than allopathic medicine to cure the human body.

Patriarchy: A system of inequality primarily based on gender, in which cisgender, heterosexual men are privileged and noncisgender, nonheterosexual people are oppressed.

Privilege: Describes both the experience of being advantaged and the absence of obstacles in achieving success and comfort in life.

Racial Hierarchy: The societal ranking of people based on race, where people lower on the hierarchy experience more discrimination and oppression. Whiteness is at the top of the hierarchy, and proximity to Whiteness can be seen as a measure of privilege.

Racial Socialization: The process by which parents teach their children about race, the racial hierarchy, and how to navigate a racialized society based on the identities they hold.

Racism: A system of inequality based on racial identity in which White, Caucasian, and European people are privileged and People of Color are oppressed.

Schema: A worldview or conceptualization of how something works, usually in reference to a client's mental representation of themselves and society.

Siddha Medicine: One of the oldest medicine systems that originated in Southern Indian, primarily taught through master-disciple relationships. This medicine is very closely guarded and not shared with just anyone. Treatments are focused on restoring equilibrium of the three humors.

Sound Meditation: Use of sounds through music or chanting to restore energetic balance in the mind and body.

Sufi Masters: Sufi masters practice a form of Islamic healing tradition called Sufism. Sufism is a type of Islamic mysticism whereby Sufi masters explore divine love and knowledge via several different practices. Sufi masters also guide and teach healers (Dervish) and the community on spirituality.

Systemic (Work): Interventions (in this context, clinical interventions) that explicitly acknowledge the impact of systems of oppression on the individual.

Triangulation/Racial Triangulation: Related to the model minority myth, the isolation of Asian Americans from other racial minorities and from the American identity. Asian Americans are perceived as more successful and less oppressed than other racial minorities but also as inferior to White people. They are additionally perceived as perpetual foreigners regardless of their immigration or citizenship status, which is not a shared experience for White people or for many other racial minorities.

Twice-Removed Immigrants: Immigrants who immigrated to another country and then immigrated to the United States.

Unani System of Medicine: This form of medicine developed in Greece and made its way to precolonial India in the medieval period. The belief is that each individual has their own distinct temperament (sanguine, choleric, phlegmatic, and melancholic), and changes in these humors result in alterations in the ailments. Practitioners will often prescribe herbs or diets that match the individual's temperament.

Varnas: Caste categories in ancient Hindu scriptures.

Vedas: Ancient Hindu scriptures that dictate norms, guidelines, and rituals of Hindu culture and way of life.

Notes

Chapter 1

1. See Indian Caste System section, this chapter.
2. More information about the historic tension between Muslims and non-Muslims across South Asia can be found in texts about British colonization of India, the division of the Indian subcontinent by religion (e.g., the India-Pakistan divide), and Hindu nationalism.
3. See section on *othering*, this chapter.
4. See Asian Indian/South Asian Queer Experiences in Suggested Readings.
5. Feminist psychology began as a recognition of differences in experiences within the gender binary but has since expanded to include and explore genders outside of the binary.
6. See the Kamasutra: Sexual Liberation versus Sexual Control section, this chapter, for information on the parallels between how queerness is linked with "Western" and separate from Indianness.

Chapter 2

1. See Othering as a Reaction to Discrimination in Chapter 1.
2. See Erikson's identity development model.
3. See information about the model minority myth in the White Supremacy in U.S. Asian Indian History section in Chapter 1.
4. Cultural capital refers to cultural knowledge and awareness that an individual possesses, which is impacted by social inequality.

5. See Both-And: Biculturality in this chapter.
6. Meeting societal expectations is also a collectivistic cultural value, meaning that there are multiple dimensions of identity development in which this may be relevant for a client.
7. Refer to Table 2.1 in this chapter.
8. See The Role of the Clinician in Chapter 5.

Chapter 3

1. *Indian caste system* is used interchangeably with *Hindu caste system* (essentially, it means the same thing because the Indian caste system originated from Hinduism scriptures).
2. Remember that colorism is a type of discrimination, like racism, that is based on skin tone. When people use skin color as a determinant of caste status, they are engaging in discrimination and perpetuating systems of oppression.
3. Some Indian cookbooks based on Hindu (vedic) principles, such as books on vegetarianism, veganism, or plant-based diet regimens, are said to have roots in casteism (alienating communities who eat meat or beef as "impure").
4. These cultural values will be explored further in Chapter 4.
5. See Chapter 1 for ways that caste markers are discovered by Asian Indians (i.e., indicators of one's caste status).
6. *Mahabharata* and *Ramayana* are two major Sanskrit (language of Hindu scriptures) epics that have had a substantial impact on the Hindu religious belief system and practices, and are often reflective of Brahmanical patriarchy.
7. This is similar to immigration trauma discussed in previous chapters. Here, we consider caste-related trauma; see Moving Therapy Beyond Mental and Emotional Health: Recognizing Social and Cultural Trauma in this chapter.
8. The extent to which a clinician focuses on insight as a therapeutic goal depends on their therapeutic orientation—some orientations, like psychodynamic theories, are more insight-oriented than others.
9. *Dowry* refers to practices in India demanding money, goods, or property in order for a matrimonial alliance to be agreed upon. It is typically demanded of the bride's family, but can also be demanded

of the groom in certain regions of India. Oftentimes, individuals with low-caste or Dalit backgrounds, as well as dark-skinned women, experience greater dowry harassment.

10. In Chapter 2, we discussed how assimilation may be a harmful goal for clinicians to endorse for their clients because of the way it promotes the loss of a culture of origin to the dominant, Western culture.

Chapter 4

1. By *language*, we are referring to literacy in English as well as knowledge of slang and idioms. Examples of unspoken cultural norms include things like voice volume and physical distance in a conversation and courtesy smiling when passing a stranger on the sidewalk. *Systems* refers to things like banking and investment, taxes, voting, and health care.
2. For a discussion of endogamy, see Chapter 1
3. *Filial piety* refers to the virtue of respect and obedience from children toward their parents, and the term is tied to Confucianism, Chinese Buddhism, and Taoism. Very similar virtues exist across cultures, and this concept is known in Asian Indian culture as *seva*. See Sharma and Kemp (2012) in Suggested Readings for further discussion.
4. See *identity diffusion* in Chapter 2 and in the glossary.
5. *Cisnormative* describes the restrictive and oppressive conceptualization of binary genders and gender roles.

Chapter 5

1. WEIRD: Western, Educated, Industrialized, Rich, and Democratic.
2. Examples of this for Asian Indians are described in Chapter 2.
3. For additional information, see Suggested Readings.
4. This phenomenon has been described in other therapies (such as psychodynamic and interpersonal therapy) as the transference/ countertransference and parallel process.

References

Ahmad, I. (1978). *Caste and social stratification among the Muslims in India*. Manohar Books.

Ahuja, K. K. (2017). Development of attitudes toward homosexuality scale for Indians (AHSI). *Journal of Homosexuality, 64*(14), 1978–1992. https://doi.org/10.1080/00918369.2017.1289006

Ali, S. (2002). Collective and elective ethnicity: Caste among urban Muslims in India. *Sociological Forum, 17*(4), 593–620. http://doi.org/10.1023/A:1021077323866

Al-Krenawi, A., & Graham, J. R. (2000). Culturally sensitive social work practice with Arab clients in mental health settings. *Health and Social Work, 25*(1), 9–22. https://doi.org/10.1093/hsw/25.1.9

AlRawi, S., Fetters, M. D., Killawi, A., Hammad, A., & Padela, A. (2011). Traditional healing practices among American Muslims: Perceptions of community leaders in Southeast Michigan. *Journal of Immigrant Mental Health, 14*(3), 489–496. https://doi.org/10.1007/s10903-011-9495-0

Ambedkar, B. R. (1948). *The Untouchables: Who were they and why they became Untouchables?* Chennai: MJP Publishers.

Azad, S. A. K., & Nayak, P. K. (2016). Health care barriers faced by LGBT people in India: An investigative study. *Research Innovator, 3*(5), 2395–4744.

Bacon, J. (1999). Constructing collective ethnic identities: The case of second generation Asian Indians. *Qualitative Sociology, 22.* https://doi.org/10.1023/A:1022024124899

Bald, V. (2013). *Bengali Harlem and the lost histories of South Asian America.* Harvard University Press.

Bansal, P. (2020). *Both, and: The dichotomous relationship between the model minority myth and psychological distress for South Asians in the United States* (Publication No. 28153575) [Master's thesis, University of Maryland]. ProQuest Dissertations & Theses Global.

Berry, J. W. (1997). Immigration, acculturation, and adaptation. *International Association of Applied Psychology, 46*(1), 5–68. https://doi.org/10.1111/j.1464-0597.1997.tb01087.x

Berry, J. W. (2003). Conceptual approaches to acculturation. In K. M. Chun, P. B. Organista, & G. Marin (Eds.), *Acculturation: Advances in theory, measurement and applied research* (pp. 17–37). American Psychological Association.

Berry, J. W. (2005). Acculturation: Living successfully in two cultures. *International Journal of Intercultural Relations, 29*(6), 697–712. https://doi.org/10.1016/j.ijintrel.2005.07.013

Berry, J. W. (2006). Acculturation: A conceptual overview. In M. H. Bornstein & L. R Cote (Eds.), *Acculturation and parent-child relationships: Measurement and development* (pp. 13–30). Lawrence Erlbaum.

Bhasin, K. (1993). *What is patriarchy.* Kali for Women.

Bhatia, S. C., Khan, M. H., Mediratta, R. P., & Sharma, A. (1987). High risk suicide factors across cultures. *International Journal of Social Psychiatry, 33*(3), 226–236. https://doi.org/10.1177/002076408703300307

Blackwell, D. (2003). Colonialism and globalization: A group-analytic perspective. *Group Analysis, 36*(4), 445–463. https://doi.org/10.1177/0533316403364002

Brigham, C. C. (1922). *A study of American intelligence.* Princeton University Press.

Burman, E. (2020). Therapy of/for the oppressed: Frantz Fanon's psychopolitical pedagogy of transformation. In L. Turner & H. Neville (Eds.), *Frantz Fanon's psychotherapeutic approaches to clinical work: Practicing internationally with marginalized communities* (pp. 109–126). Routledge.

Caldwell, J. C., Reddy, P. H., & Caldwell, P. (1984). The determinants of family structure in rural south India. *Journal of Marriage and the Family, 46*(1), 215–229. https://doi.org/10.2307/351879

Chadda, R., & Deb, K. (2013). Indian family systems, collectivistic society and psychotherapy. *Indian Journal of Psychiatry, 55*, 299–309. https://doi.org/10.4103/0019-5545.105555

Chakravorty, S., Goli, S., & James, K. S. (2021). Family demography in India: Emerging patterns and its challenges. *Sage Open, (11)*2. https://doi.org/10.1177/21582440211008178

Chan, W., & Mendoza-Denton, R. (2008). Status-based rejection sensitivity among Asian Americans: Implications for psychological distress. *Journal of Personality, 76*(5), 1317–1346. https://doi.org/10.1111/j.1467-6494.2008.00522.x

Chang, H. (2017). *The internalization of the model minority stereotype, acculturative stress, and ethnic identity on academic stress, academic performance, and mental health among Asian American college students.* (Publication No. 2785). [Doctoral dissertation, Loyola University Chicago]. Dissertations.

Chavez-Dueñas, N. Y., Adames, H. Y., Perez-Chavez, J. G., & Salas, S. P. (2019). Healing ethno-racial trauma in Latinx immigrant communities: Cultivating hope, resistance, and action. *American Psychologist, 74*(1), 49–62. https://doi.org/10.1037/amp0000289

Crenshaw, K. (1989). Demarginalizing the intersection of race and sex: Black feminist critique of antidiscrimination doctrine, feminist theory and antiracist politics. *University of Chicago Legal Forum*, 139–168.

Daga, S. S., & Raval, V. V. (2018). Ethnic-racial socialization, model minority experience, and psychological functioning among South Asian American emerging adults: A preliminary mixed-methods study. *Asian American Journal of Psychology, 9*(1), 17–31. https://doi.org/10.1037/aap0000108

Dalal, A. K. (2007). Folk wisdom and traditional healing practices: Some lessons for modern psychotherapies. In M. Cornelisson, G. Misra, & S. Verma (Eds.), *Foundations of Indian Psychology.* Pearson.

Das, A. K., & Kemp, S. F. (1997). Between two worlds: Counseling South Asian Americans. *Journal of Multicultural Counseling and Development, 25*(1), 23–33. https://doi.org/10.1002/j.2161-1912.1997.tb00313.x

Dube, L. (1996). Caste and women. In M. N. Srinivas (Ed.), *Caste: Its twentieth century avatar* (pp. 1–27). Penguin.

Du Bois, W. E. B. (1903). *The souls of Black folk.* Penguin.

Duran, E., Firehammer, J., & Gonzalez, J. (2008). Liberation psychology as the path toward healing cultural soul wounds. *Journal of Counseling and Development, 86*(3), 288–295. https://doi.org/10.1002/j.1556-6678.2008.tb00511.x

Duran, B. and E. Duran (2000). Applied postcolonial clinical and research strategies. In M. Battiste (Ed.), *Reclaiming Indigenous voice and vision* (pp 86-100). UBC Press.

Durvasula, R. S., & Mylvaganam, G. A. (1994). Mental health of Asian Indians: Relevant issues and community implications. *Journal of Community Psychology, 22*(2), 97–108. https://doi.org/10.1002/1520-6629(199404)22:2%3C97::AID-JCOP2290220206%3E3.0.CO;2-%23

Ejaz, K., & Moscowitz, L. (2020). Who "framed" Ramchandra Siras? Journalistic discourses of sexual citizenship in India. *Sexualities, 23*(5–6), 951–970. https://doi.org/10.1177%2F1363460719876829

Erikson, E. H. (1968). *Identity, youth and crisis.* W. W. Norton.

Falk, J., Hampton, G. R., Hodgkinson, A. T., Parker, K., & Rorris, A. (1993). *Social equity and the urban environment: Report to the Commonwealth Environment Protection Agency.* Australian Government Publishing Service.

Foelsch P.A., Odom A, & Kernberg O.F. (2008). Treatment of adolescents with identity diffusion: A modification of transference focused psychotherapy. *Sante Ment Que, 33*(1), 37-60. https://doi.org/ 10.7202/018472ar

Gairola, R. K. (2017) Bastardly duppies and dastardly dykes: Queer sexuality and the supernatural in Michelle Cliff's Abeng (1984) and Shani Mootoo's Cereus Blooms at Night (1996). *Wagadu: A Journal of Transnational Women's and Gender Studies, 18*, 15–54. Retrieved from http://researchrepository.murdoch.edu.au/id/eprint/51959

Galton, F. (1883). *Inquiries into human faculty and its development.* Macmillan.

Garcia, G. M., David, E. J. R., & Mapaye, J. C. (2019). Internalized racial oppression as a moderator of the relationship between experiences of racial discrimination and mental distress among Asians and Pacific Islanders. *American Psychological Association, 10*(2), 103–112. https://doi.org/10.1037/aap0000124

Geetha, V. (2007). *Patriarchy.* Stree.

Gone, J. P. (2008). Introduction: Mental health discourse as Western cultural proselytization. *Ethos, 36*(3), 310–315. https://doi.org/10.1111/j.1548-1352.2008.00016.x

Gopinath, G. (2005). *Impossible desires.* Duke University Press.

Goth, K., Foelsch, P., Schlüter-Müller, S., Birkhölzer, M., Jung, E., Pick, O., & Schmeck, K. (2012). Assessment of identity development and identity diffusion in adolescence: Theoretical basis and psychometric properties of the self-report questionnaire AIDA. *Child and Adolescent Psychiatry and Mental Health, 6*, Article 27. http://doi.org/10.1186/1753-2000-6-27

Gupta, A. (2005). Englishpur ki kothi: Class dynamics in queer movement in India. In A. Narrain & G. Bhan (Eds.), *Because I have a voice: Queer politics in India* (pp. 123–42). Yoda Press.

Gupta, A. (2006). Section 377 and dignity of Indian homosexuals. *Economic and Political Weekly, 41*(46), 4815–4823. Retrieved from https://jcil.lsyndicate.com/wp-content/uploads/2018/08/Section-377-Is-It-Needed-For-India-18.pdf

Gupta, A., Szymanski, D. M., & Leong, F. T. L. (2011). The "model minority myth": Internalized racialism of positive stereotypes as correlates of psychological distress, and attitudes toward help-seeking. *Asian American Journal of Psychology, 2*(2), 101–114. https://doi.org/10.1037/a0024183

Gupta, P., Sharma, K. V., & Sharma, S. (2014). *Healing traditions of the Northwestern Himalayas.* Springer.

Heatherington, L., Messer, S. B., Angus, L., Strauman, T. J., Friedlander, M. L., & Kolden, G. G. (2012). The narrowing of theoretical orientations in clinical psychology doctoral training. *Clinical Psychology: Science and Practice, 19*(4), 364–374. https://doi.org/10.1111/cpsp.12012

Henrich, J., Heine, S., & Norenzayan, A. (2010). The weirdest people in the world? *Behavioral and Brain Sciences, 33*(2–3), 61–83. https://doi.org/10.1017/S0140525X0999152X

Herskovits, M. J. (1948). *Man and his works: The science of cultural anthropology.* Knopf.

Hess, G. (1969). The "Hindu" in America: Immigration and naturalization policies and India, 1917–1946. *Pacific Historical Review, 38*(1), 59–79. https://doi.org/10.2307/3636886

Horney, K. (1993). *Feminine psychology.* W. W. Norton.

Horse, P. G. (2005), Native American identity. *New Directions for Student Services, 2005*(109), 61–68. https://doi.org/10.1002/ss.154

Hossain, A. (2017). The paradox of recognition: hijra, third gender and sexual rights in Bangladesh. *Culture, Health & Sexuality: An International Journal for Research, Intervention and Care, 19*(12). https://doi.org/10.1080/1369105 8.2017.1317831

Ibrahim, F., Ohnishi, H., & Sandhu, D. S. (1997). Asian American identity development: A culture specific model for South Asian Americans. *Journal of Multicultural Counseling and Development, 25*(1), 34–50. https://doi.org/10.1002/j.2161-1912.1997.tb00314.x

Iwamoto, D. K., & Liu, W. M. (2010). The impact of racial identity, ethnic identity, Asian values and race-related stress on Asian Americans and Asian international college students' psychological well-being. *Journal of Counseling Psychology, 57*(1), 79–91. https://doi.org/10.1037/a0017393

Iyer, D. (2015). *We too sing America: South Asian, Arab, Muslim, and Sikh immigrants shape our multiracial future.* New Press.

Johansson, P. M., & Punzi, E. (2019). Jewishness and psychoanalysis: The relationship to identity, trauma and exile; An interview study. *Jewish Culture and History, 20*(2), 140–152. https://doi.org/10.1080/1462169X.2019.1574429

Kakar, S. (1982). *Shamans, mystics and doctors.* Oxford University Press.

Kapoor, D. (2007). Gendered-caste discrimination, human rights education, and the enforcement of the Prevention of Atrocities Act in India. *Alberta Journal of Educational Research, 53*(3), 273–286. https://doi.org/10.11575/ajer.v53i3.55293

Kim, B. S. K., & Abreu, J. M. (2001). *Acculturation measurement: Theory, current instruments, and future directions.* In J. G. Ponterotto, J. M. Casas, L. A. Suzuki, & C. M. Alexander (Eds.), *Handbook of multicultural counseling* (pp. 394–424). Sage.

Kim, C. J. (1999). The racial triangulation of Asian Americans. *Politics and Society, 27*(1), 105–138. https://doi.org/10.1177/0032329299027001005

Kim, J. E., & Zane, N. (2016). Help-seeking intentions among Asian American and White American students in psychological distress: *Application of the health belief model*. *Cultural Diversity and Ethnic Minority Psychology, 22*(3), 311–321. https://doi.org/10.1037/cdp0000056

Kumar, M., Bhugra, D., & Singh, J. (2005). South Asian (Indian) traditional healing: Ayurvedic, shamanic, and sahaja therapy. In R. Moodley & W. West (Eds.), *Integrating traditional healing practices into counseling and psychotherapy* (pp. 112–121). Sage. https://doi.org/10.4135/9781452231648.n10

Kumar, P. (2008, November 3–7). *Disordered body in Middle Town* [Paper presentation]. International Conference on Interrogating South Asian Masculinity, Bellagio, Italy.

Kumar, P. (2009, July 6–7). *"What gain, what pain": Small town kothis, metropolitan hijras and emerging bodily practices in western India* [Paper presentation]. International Workshop on Globalisation in/on Mofussil India. London School of Economics and Political Science.

Kuriloff, E. A. (2014). *Contemporary psychoanalysis and the legacy of the Third Reich: History, memory, tradition*. Routledge.

Lara-Cinisomo, S., Akinbode, T. D., & Wood, J. (2020). A systematic review of somatic symptoms in women with depression or depressive symptoms: Do race or ethnicity matter? *Journal of Women's Health, 29*(10), 1273–1282. https://doi.org/10.1089/jwh.2019.7975

Lee, M. M., & Navarro, A. (2018). Prioritizing racial equity: How efforts to advance racial equity helped shape the W. K. Kellogg Food and Fitness Initiative. *Health Promotion Practice, 19*(1), 24S–33S. https://doi.org/10.1177%2F1524839918783970

Leung, P., Cheung, M., & Tsui, V. (2011). Asian Indians and depressive symptoms: Reframing mental health help-seeking behavior. *International Social Work, 55*(1), 53–70. https://doi.org/10.1177%2F0020872811407940

Malhotra, H. K., Inam, A. S., & Chopra, H. D. (1981). Do the psychiatric patients reject themselves? *Indian Journal of Psychiatry, 23*(1), 44–48.

Mallinson, S., & Popay, J. (2007). Describing depression: Ethnicity and the use of somatic imagery in accounts of mental distress. *Sociology of Health and Illness, 29*(6), 857–871. https://doi.org/10.1111/j.1467-9566.2007.01048.x

Mancino, J. (2019, June 1). Hijra: Inside the lives of India's secretive transgender minority. *Jetset Times.* https://jetsettimes.com/lgbtq/hijra/

Mankekar, P. (2004). Dangerous desires: Televisions and erotic in late twentieth century India. *Journal of Asian Studies, 63*(2), 403–431. http://www.jstor.org/stable/4133391

Menon, N. (Ed.). (2007). *Sexualities*. Women Unlimited.

Miller, M. J., Yang, M., Farrell, J. A., & Lin, L. (2011). Racial and cultural factors affecting the mental health of Asian Americans. *American Journal of Orthopsychiatry, 81*(4), 489–497. https://doi.org/10.1111/j.1939-0025.2011.01118.x

Museus, S. D., & Park, J. (2015). The continuing significance of racism in the lives of Asian American college students. *Journal of College Student Development, 56*(6), 551–569. https://doi.org/ 10.1353/csd.2015.0059

Nambiar, S. (2017, January 1). *A brief history of Hijra, India's third gender*. Culture Trip. https://theculturetrip.com/asia/india/articles/a-brief-history-of-hijra-indias-third-gender/

Nanda, S. (1999). *Neither man or woman: The Hijras of India*. Wadsworth.

Nikalje, A., & Çiftçi, A. (2021). Colonial mentality, racism, and depressive symptoms: Asian Indians in the United States. *Asian American Journal of Psychology*. Advance online publication. https://doi.org/10.1037/aap0000262

Obergefell v. Hodges, 576 U.S. ___ (2015). https://www.supremecourt.gov/opinions/14pdf/14-556_3204.pdf

Osajima, K. (1993). The hidden injuries of race. In L. Revilla, G. Nomura, S. Wong, & S. Hune (Eds.), *Bearing dreams, shaping visions: Asian Pacific American perspectives* (pp. 81–91). Washington State University Press.

Panghal, M., Arya, V., Yadav, S., Kumar, S., & Yadav, J. P. (2010). Indigenous knowledge of medicinal plants used by Saperas community of Khetawas, Jhajjar District, Haryana, India. *Journal of Ethnobiology and Ethnomedicine, 6*(4). https://doi.org/10.1186/1746-4269-6-4

Paul, S. (2018, April 25). When caste discrimination comes to the United States. NPR. https://www.npr.org/sections/codeswitch/2018/04/25/605030018/when-caste-discrimination-comes-to-the-united-states

Pescosolido, B. A., & Boyer, C. A. (1999). How do people come to use mental health services? Current knowledge and changing perspectives. In A. V. Horwitz & T. L. Scheid *(Eds.), A handbook for the study of mental health: social contexts, theories, and systems* (pp. 392–411). Cambridge University Press.

Peterson, W. (1966, December 26). Success story of one minority group in the U.S. *U.S. News and World Report, 73*–78.

Puri, H. K. (2003). Scheduled castes in Sikh community: A historical perspective. *Economic and Political Weekly, 38*(26), 2693–2701.

Pyke, K. D. (2010). What is internalized racial oppression and why don't we study it? Acknowledging racism's hidden injuries. *Sociological Perspectives, 53*(4), 551–572. https://doi.org/10.1525/sop.2010.53.4.551

Rajiva, M. (2006). Brown girls, White worlds: Adolescence and the making of racialized selves. *Canadian Review of Sociology and Anthropology, 43*(2), 165–183. https://doi.org/10.1111/j.1755-618x.2006.tb02218.x

Reddy, D. S. (2005). The ethnicity of caste. *University of Houston–Clear Lake Anthropological Quarterly, 78*(3), 543–584.

Rose, A. L., & Cheung, M. (2012) DSM-5 research: Assessing the mental health needs of older adults from diverse ethnic backgrounds. *Journal of Ethnic and Cultural Diversity in Social Work, 21*(2), 144–167. https://doi.org/10.1080/15 313204.2012.673437

Schwalbe, M., Godwin, S., Holden, D., Schrock, D., Thompson, S., & Wolkomir, M. (2000). Generic processes in the reproduction of inequality: An interactionist analysis. *Social Forces, 79*(2), 419–452. https://doi.org/10.2307/2675505

Segal, U. A. (1991). Cultural variables in Asian Indian families. Families in Society: *Journal of Contemporary Human Services, 72*(4), 233–242. https://doi.org/10.1177/104438949107200406

Segal, U. A. (1998). The Asian Indian-American family. In C. H. Mindel, R. W. Habenstein, & R. Wright Jr. (Eds.), *Ethnic families in America: Patterns and variation* (4th ed.). Prentice-Hall.

Shah, H. (1999). Race, nation, and citizenship: Asian Indians and the idea of whiteness in the U.S. press, 1906–1923. *Howard Journal of Communication, 10*(4), 249–267. https://doi.org/10.1080/106461799246744

Singh, S. R. (2020, June 11). *#DalitLivesMatter: Why are atrocities against Dalits on the rise?* Feminism in India. https://feminisminindia.com/2020/06/11/dalitlivesmatter-atrocities-against-dalits-increase/

Soorkia, R., Snelgar, R., & Swami, V. (2011). Factors influencing attitudes towards seeking professional psychological help among South Asian students in Britain. *Mental Health, Religion and Culture, 14*(6), 613–623. https://doi.org/10.1080/13674676.2010.494176

Sue, D. W. (1994). Asian-American mental health and help-seeking behavior: Comment on Solberg et al. (1994), Tata and Leong (1994), and Lin (1994). *Journal of Counseling Psychology, 41*(3), 292–295. https://doi.org/10.1037/0022-0167.41.3.292

Sue, S., & Morishima, J. (1982). *The mental health of Asian Americans.* Jossey-Bass.

Szczepanski, K. (2020, February 24). *History of India's caste system.* ThoughtCo. https://www.thoughtco.com/history-of-indias-caste-system-195496

Tajfel, H., & Turner, J. C. (1979). An integrative theory of intergroup conflict. In W. G. Austin & S. Worchel (Eds.), *The social psychology of intergroup relations* (pp. 33–37). Brooks/Cole.

Tatum, B. D. (1997). *Why are the Black kids sitting together in the cafeteria?* HarperCollins.

Tummala-Narra, P., Deshpande, A., & Kaur, J. (2016). South Asian adolescents' experiences of acculturative stress and coping. *Journal of Adolescent Research*, *31*(3), 299–342. https://doi.org/10.1177/0743558415592178

United States v. Bhagat Singh Thind, 261 U.S. 204 (1923). https://supreme.justia.com/cases/federal/us/261/204/

Walby, S. (1990). *Theorizing patriarchy*. Basil Blackwell.

Wilkerson, I. (2020, July 1). *America's enduring caste system*. The New York Times. https://www.nytimes.com/2020/07/01/magazine/isabel-wilkerson-caste.html?auth=logingoogle1tap&login=google1tap&referringSource=articleShare

Wong, P., Lai, C. F., Nagasawa, R., & Lin, T. (1998). Asian Americans as a model minority: Self-perceptions and perceptions by other racial groups. *Sociological Perspectives*, *41*(1), 95–118. https://doi.org/10.2307/1389355

Zaidi, A. U., & Shuraydi, M. (2002). Perceptions of arranged marriages by young Pakistani Muslim women living in a Western society. *Journal of Family and Comparative Studies*, *33*(4), 495–514. https://www.jstor.org/stable/41603839

Zwick-Maitreyi, M., Soundararajan, T., Dar, N., Bheel, R. F., & Balakrishnan, P. (2018). *Caste in the United States: A survey of caste Among South Asian Americans*. Equality Labs. https://www.equalitylabs.org/castesurvey

Suggested Readings

Indian Caste System

Ahmad, A. S. (2015, April 21). *How to fight a deadly caste system.* Colorlines. https://www.colorlines.com/articles/how-fight-deadly-caste-system

Ambedkar, B. R. (1936). *Annihilation of caste.*

Ambedkar, B. R. (1948). *The Untouchables: Who were they and why they became Untouchables?* MJP Publishers.

Immerwahr, D. (2007). Caste or colony? Indianizing race in the United States. *Modern Intellectual History, 4*(2), 275–301. https://doi.org/10.1017/S1479244307001205

Jadhav, N. (2007). *Untouchables: My family's triumphant escape from India's caste system.* University of California Press.

Soundararajan, T. (2012, August 20). *The Black Indians: Growing up Dalit in the US, finding your roots, fighting for your identity.* Outlook India. https://magazine.outlookindia.com/story/the-black-indians/281938

Valmiki, O. (2008). *Joothan: An Untouchable's life* (A. P. Mukherjee, Trans). Columbia University Press.

Zwick-Maitreyi, M., Soundararajan, T., Dar, N., Bheel, R. F., & Balakrishnan, P. (2018). *Caste in the United States. A survey of caste among South Asian Americans.* Equality Labs. https://www.equalitylabs.org/castesurvey

Asian Indian/South Asian Queer Experiences

Bannerji, K. (1993). *No apologies.* In R. Ratti (Ed.), *A lotus of another color: An unfolding of the South Asian gay and lesbian experience* (pp. 59–64). Alyson.

Gopinath, G. (1996). Funny boys and girls: Notes on a Queer South Asian planet. In R. Leong (Ed.), *Asian American sexualities: Dimensions of the gay and lesbian experience.* Routledge.

Gopinath, G. (2005). *Impossible desires: Queer diasporas and South Asian public cultures.* Duke University Press.

Nanda, S. (1999). *Neither man nor woman: The Hijras of India.* Wadsworth.

Filial Piety

Sharma, K., & Kemp, C. L. (2012). "One should follow the wind": Individualized filial piety and support exchanges in Indian immigrant families in the United States. *Journal of Aging Studies, 26*(2), 129–139. https://doi.org/10.1016/j.jaging.2011.10.003

Ancient Asian Indian Healing Practices

AlRawi, S., Fetters, M. D., Killawi, A., Hammad, A., & Padela, A. (2011). Traditional healing practices among American Muslims: Perceptions of community leaders in Southeast Michigan. *Journal of Immigrant Mental Health, 14*(3), 489–496. https://doi.org/10.1007/s10903-011-9495-0

Flueckiger, J. B. (2006). *In Amma's healing room: Gender and vernacular Islam in South India.* Indiana University Press.

Gupta, P., Sharma, K. V., & Sharma, S. (2014). *Healing traditions of the Northwestern Himalayas.* Springer.

Kakar, S. (1982). *Shamans, mystics and doctors.* Oxford University Press.

Karthigayan, P. (2016). *History of medical and spiritual sciences of Siddhas of Tamil Nadu.* Notion Press.

Panghal, M., Arya, V., Yadav, S., Kumar, S., & Yadav, J. P. (2010). Indigenous knowledge of medicinal plants used by Saperas community of Khetawas, Jhajjar District, Haryana, India. *Journal Ethnobiology and Ethnomedicine, 6*(4), Article No. 4. https://doi.org/10.1186/1746-4269-6-4

Shankar, R., Lavekar, G. S., Deb, S., & Sharma, B. K. (2012). Traditional healing practice and folk medicines used by Mishing community of North East India. *Journal of Ayurveda and Integrative Medicine, 3*(3), 124–129. https://doi.org/10.4103/0975-9476.100171

Asian Indian Mental Health and Treatment

Rao, V. A., Juthani, N. V., & Peters, M. E. (2019). *Mental illness among South Asian Americans: Twenty culturally mindful case studies.* iUniverse.

Roysircar, G., & Lanza, A. (2021). *People of Color: Casebook of clinical considerations.*

Asian Indian Identity/Asian Indian Experiences

Deonath, G., & Ramdeen, K. (2021). *Untold: Defining moments of the uprooted.* Mango and Marigold Press.

Hasan, Z. (1994). *Forging identities: Gender, communities, and state in India.* Routledge.

Sarkar, S. (2008). *Desi land teen culture, class, and success in Silicon Valley.* Duke University Press.

Index

W

WEIRD population, 104
Western cultures, 27, 37, 93
Western-informed boundaries, 52
Westernized cultural norms and traditions, 47
Western psychological frameworks, 59, 113
Western systems of patriarchy, 25–26
White American culture, 59–60
White cultural norm, 46
Whiteness, 84
White supremacy, 6–8, 13, 15–16, 19, 23, 59–61, 103–104
World War II, 7

X

xenophobia, 8

Y

yoga therapy, 106

About the Authors

Sonia Amin, Ph.D., is a 1.5 generation, Zimbabwean-born and Asian Indian descent, multilingual, cis-gender woman. She obtained her master of arts degree in clinical psychology from the University of Detroit Mercy and her doctoral degree in counseling psychology from Western Michigan University. Dr. Amin completed her doctoral internship and post doctoral fellowship at University of California–Berkeley's Counseling and Psychological Services with a special focus on outreach for underserved student communities, systemic racial inequalities, and decolonizing mental health practices. Her clinical experiences include college counseling centers, integrated behavioral health settings, and community clinics. Her research interests include bicultural identity conflicts, decolonizing mental health and liberatory healing practices, intergenerational trauma, racial and sexual identity development, and radical self-healing.

Priya Bansal, M.A. is a doctoral candidate for counseling psychology at the University of Maryland, College Park, where she also obtained her master of arts degree in counseling psychology. She identifies as a second-generation Indian American, bisexual, cisgender woman and is Hindi-English bilingual. Her research focuses on decolonization of the practice of psychotherapy, navigating systems of oppression, and identity development and mental health correlates for South Asians in the United States. She centers social justice advocacy in her research, clinical, and personal work. Priya's clinical experiences include trauma-informed short-term and long-term psychotherapy in nonprofit and community settings.

CPSIA information can be obtained
at www.ICGtesting.com
Printed in the USA
LVHW080713200422
716652LV00002B/18